The Enchiridion of Aquarius
A New Living Handbook

The Enchiridion of Aquarius

A New Living Handbook

First Edition

AUCTOR

NEW LIVING CLASSICS

NEW LIVING CLASSICS

Published in the United States by
New Living Foundation
1621 Central Avenue
Cheyenne, Wyoming 82001

NewLivingFoundation.org

First edition published as a paperback in 2016.

Copyright © 2016 by Auctor.
All rights reserved.

No part of this publication may be reproduced or transmitted in any
form or by any means without written permission from the publisher,
except that reviewers may quote brief passages.

This edition may be printed on demand, which may result in
variance in the trim and alignment of the cover and interior pages.

ISBN-10: 0998253103
ISBN-13: 978-0998253107

*For my own spirit
and kindred seekers*

Contents

Preface
Theses   10

Introduction
Overture   16
Glossary   18

Exposition
Manifesto   22
Proviso   28
Credo   32

The Meta-Spiritual Matrix
Universal Flow   38
Hope   41
Realms Outer   46
Realms Inner   49
Chasm   53
Crossing   56
Chaos & Kosmos   59
Taxis & Telos   61
Deliverance   64
Psyche   68
Dimensions   71
Foundation   74

Trans-Spiritual Invariants
Emergence   80
Paradigms   82

Physics of Sky	84
Physics of Sea	86
Physics of Land	88
Ethics	91

A New Living Tradition

Tree of Life	96
Sunlight	100
Rain	103
Breath	105
Soil	107
Gardener	109
Entelechy	113
Temple & Altar	115
Garden of Life	118

Conclusion

Testament	122
Codicil	124

PREFACE

THESES
Reformation & Restoration

Recent years have witnessed something remarkable: A renewal of interest in forms of spirituality inspired by beliefs and practices from long ago that we, humankind collectively, had thought extinct, prompting (I would argue) the promotion of an otherwise common noun originally intended as a pejorative to the ranks of proper nouns that name religions: Paganism.

The reemergence of Paganism (also called "Neopaganism" to distinguish this new branch from its "Mesopagan" trunk and their "Paleopagan" roots) has given rise to countless diverse traditions that seem yet to share certain core features, in particular, a respect for timeless human wisdom and a distinctive appreciation of and reverence for the natural world.

Beyond this core, however, Neopaganism splits itself between two antipodal approaches: Reconstructionists attempt to recreate Paleopagan and Mesopagan religions whole, while Eclectics select and combine disparate components from an assortment of Pagan—sometimes even non-Pagan—religions.

One could say that Reconstructionism was the Neopagan thesis that Gerald Gardner first advanced, however implicitly, in his landmark *Witchcraft Today* (1954), which thesis soon gave rise to its antithesis, Eclecticism.

Now the time has come for a new dispensation, a synthesis that will transcend and supersede the antipodes that have precipitated it: Reformism.

I come thus to a thesis of my own: The future of Neopaganism lies in neither Reconstructionism nor Eclecticism but Reformism, which will take the form of a Pagan Reformation and a new branch of the Pagan tree, Reform Paganism, which itself will blossom in new Neopagan traditions distinct from Reconstructionist and Eclectic traditions alike.

And the Pagan Reformation will proclaim certain ancillary theses, which I may be the first to formulate as such:

Naturalism: Reform Paganism grows from deep and inseverable roots in nature, which is, however proximately or distantly, the progenitor of all human religion.

Humanism: Reform Paganism promotes human flourishing (eudaimonia) within nature, for human religion should serve no other purpose.

Eternalism: Reform Paganism regards not only the human past, as all Neopagans do, but also the human, transhuman, and post-human future, rejoicing at the accelerating advancement of science and technology.

Realism: Reform Paganism pursues truth in all its aspects, embracing wonder at that which exceeds our present understanding, openness to new ideas, methodological skepticism, and active investigation of the world around us.

Transcendentalism: Reform Paganism finds that spiritual truth is transcendent, its essence and fullness irreducible to words, formulas, or teachings—every human person must ultimately obtain spiritual truth, if at all, not through the mediation of any supposed authority but by direct experience alone.

Exotericism: Reform Paganism reveals spiritual truth radically to all, neither hiding nor reserving anything from any earnest seeker but rending all false veils.

Syncretism: Reform Paganism gathers the scattered seeds of human wisdom from all spiritual traditions and secular fields of learning, not merely to compile a collection (Eclecticism) but rather to make from them something new.

Nonsectarianism (Universalism): Reform Paganism aligns itself with no divisive sect or cause but opens and offers—even recommends—itself to all.

Egalitarianism: Reform Paganism demands no initiation or ordination of any person but regards all of us as inherently equal and equally qualified in matters of spirit.

Integrationism: Reform Paganism unites all people and encourages adherents actively to integrate themselves into the world, rather than to separate themselves from it.

Ritualism: Reform Paganism celebrates events, however momentous or commonplace, in nature and human life, using rituals to deepen our experience of these special and periodic occasions.

Mysticism: Reform Paganism embraces altered states of consciousness, particularly those attained through meditative practices, and explores all the depths and heights of the human psyche, considering mystical experience essential to a complete spiritual life.

Holism: Reform Paganism informs, guides, and enlivens the entire person, soma and psyche, as spirituality is a worldview and lifeway.

Regenerationism: Reform Paganism lives and must grow and adapt as much as individual human persons live and must grow and adapt—reform and renewal are never finished.

Missionalism: Reform Paganism yokes itself with a loving mission to advance its own causes for the benefit of all humankind and all of nature, for Reform Paganism is a unique culmination and fulfillment of human spirituality, even of the development of the very noosphere.

The sooner Neopagans appreciate and accept the necessity and inevitability of the Pagan Reformation, including the evolution of a new Reform Pagan family of traditions, the faster Paganism will grow and spread, bringing us closer to another phase in the development of this religion that may yet follow: Restoration.

So I offer this work and its New Living Tradition as not only a call to Reformation but also a first example of a Reform Pagan path, all in the hope that Neopagans might begin a conversation that leads to the continuing development and growth of our religion.

Introduction

Overture
From the Author

My primary motivation in creating *The Enchiridion of Aquarius: A New Living Handbook* has been to launch a Reform Pagan tradition that promotes the Autopoiesis of the Universe in four Dimensions, under four Impulses: Perfection of human spirits, Exaltation of humankind in transhumanity, Succession of spiritual Dispensations, and Propagation of Apokalypsis as Didakhe.

For continuing Autopoiesis of the Universe in these four Dimensions, under these four Impulses, draws an ever-greater number of persons to ever-greater degrees of Eudaimonia.

The meaning of the preceding paragraphs will be obscure to anyone unfamiliar with the contents of this work, so I might, for purposes of an introduction, say rather:

This work shares certain things I have discovered in my spiritual journey and quest that have become priceless treasures in my own life; I hope that the sharing of my testimony will promote fourfold spiritual development: of individual persons who put what I relate herein to the test, of the material conditions of our species, of our spiritual traditions away from delusion and nearer unto Truth (even by subjecting my own testimony to the honing and polishing influences of criticism), and of our shared awareness and understanding.

The Universe unfolds unceasingly and ineluctably in a great drama of self-creation, Autopoiesis.

From cosmogenesis to biogenesis to noogenesis, organization builds upon itself, the system's complexity and information increasing in magnitude and at an increasing rate.

This process has brought us to the very precipice of, and will presently emerge onto, a new level: theogenesis, the creation by humankind of the Singularity, an integrated intelligence that will embrace us all and become like the imagined omniscient God of our past.

Even as we approach this splendorous dawn, however, we live in the waning matutinal hours of the human era, when the religions and spiritualities that reinforced the humanity of former ages are retreating, even withdrawing altogether, in the face of the cleansing forces of inquiry and progress that disenchant all of Nature's Creation.

Many of us are losing and have already lost this important inheritance, while only some of us have discovered and are discovering the new spiritualities offered by the present.

This de-spiritualization is a profound tragedy, for spirituality is the very source of spirit, and loss of spirituality equates to loss of spirit, even of the entire noosphere.

I fear that the spiritual space that still remains within each person living in this late age, if voided and left a vacuum, may fill with many new and contagious delusions that carry the potential to precipitate humankind's own destruction.

But I have faith that this specter of great and final apostasy, the dark and towering storm cloud that gathers already on the horizon, may yet pass us by, and I hope that my testimony both shows why and provides an example of how—one Reform Pagan spiritual path by which—we can, by embracing and fostering continued spiritual development in all its Dimensions, avoid the damning fate that may otherwise befall us if we suffer ourselves to lapse into individual and collective unspirituality.

Then can we watch with hope for a Pagan Restoration while dawn breaks bright and clear on the era of transhumanity.

This work began to germinate in my own spirit about four years ago, but the growth has been uneven, requiring long and laborious pruning to create the present text, which is still very much alive and in a continuous process of growth and renewal.

I expect that, as I grow more in my own spirituality, my testimony will develop and change; accordingly, I expect to continue to correct, revise, and improve this work in new editions.

Glossary
Terms & Definitions

Throughout this work, capitalized terms depart from their everyday usage.

Where I have chosen capitalized terms in English, I have done so specifically to allude to counterparts in common parlance, so I hope that the meanings of these terms will be clear from context.

Certain concepts, however, are absent from or not easily expressed in English proper (or are more concisely or precisely expressed in other languages); for these I have borrowed foreign terminology, particularly from certain ancient dialects of Greek, though I have adapted the meanings thereof for my own purposes.

I am providing definitions below of certain terms whose meanings specific to this work may not be apparent from context.

Acedia—willful refusal to seek after Truth; compare with "Agnoia".

Agnoia—unwitting ignorance as to Truth; compare with "Acedia".

Aletheia—revealed Truth that is immanent and immediately accessible in all of Nature, yet that is also transcendent.

Apokalypsis—propositional insight into Truth received directly and intuitively; compare with "Gnosis" and "Suneidesis".

Apokatastasis—restoration (particularly, of a person) to fullness in Nature.

Autopoiesis—unfolding and development (particularly, of the entire Universe).

Bodhi—state of spiritual attainment that implies utmost freedom from Agnoia; synonym for "Daigo".

Didakhe—Apokalypsis conveyed orally or in writing from the spirit who received it to another spirit.

Dogma, Dogmata—propositional assertion(s) to be accepted and believed without questioning; contrast with "Kerygma".

Eudaimonia—living "the good life"; human flourishing (particularly, self-actualization).

Gnosis—non-propositional insight into external Truth received directly and intuitively; compare with "Suneidesis".

Hagneia—state of spiritual attainment that implies utmost freedom from Hamartias.

Hamartia—cognition and/or behavior that impedes a person's attainment and enjoyment of Eudaimonia.

Hyle—that of which everything in Spacetime consists (namely, matter and energy in the physical Universe).

Katartisis—continuing development (particularly, spiritual) above and beyond accomplishment of Apokatastasis.

Kathairesis—dismantling (particularly, of the entire Universe into a final state of barren entropy).

Katharsis—Purgation of imperfections (particularly, Agnoia and Hamartias).

Kerygma, Kerygmata—propositional exhortation(s) to be considered for the Fruit they yield; contrast with "Dogma".

Kosmos—force and state of order produced more proximately by Nature than by any agent; contrast with "Taxis".

Memesis—force by which memes reproduce and spread in the noosphere (not to be confused with "mimesis").

Metanoia—change from Hamartias toward Hagneia, linked with obtainment of Suneidesis.

Phronema—lifestyle and mindset, built through Metanoia and Theoria, that enables enjoyment of Eudaimonia.

Suneidesis—non-propositional insight into internal Truth received directly and intuitively; compare with "Gnosis".

Taxis—force and state of order produced more proximately by an agent than by Nature; contrast with "Kosmos".

Teleosis—fulfillment of purpose or objective (particularly, human Perfection).

Theoria—change from Agnoia toward Bodhi, linked with obtainment of Gnosis.

Exposition

MANIFESTO
Overview of the Work

This work is merely a record of my personal testimony, my Kerygma, imperfect and limited, of the Eternal Order, which is Nature, Physis, the Om, the Absolute, Unus Mundus, the One All, ultimate Truth, Prakriti and Purusha, Alpha and Omega, Multiverse of possible worlds, and which is the meta-spiritual Matrix; of how Nature, as meta-spiritual Matrix, gives rise to certain trans-spiritual Invariants: the Sublime and Humane Principles of the Physics and the Ethics, lenses through which hidden spiritual wonders become apparent as Apokalypsis; of the cardinal forces that enrich spiritual life, which are the Divine Dynamics: Divine Theology and its application in Divine Spirituality (the Calculus and the Craft), supported by Divine Economy; and of the embodiment of all of the foregoing in a New Living Tradition that leads to Gnosis and Suneidesis rising unto Phronema (a worldview and lifestyle of adherence to Wisdom and the Way) and that occasions spiritual development in all Dimensions, symbolized by the growth of the Tree of Life within a person and of the Garden of Life within the human community to yield the one true fruit of the spirit, the Fruit of Life, Eudaimonia.

As to Nature, the words of my Didakhe are mere shadows, pale and indistinct, of a certain few rays of the light of Truth, neither the whole nor any part of which can be verbalized, for Truth is not of words.

As to the New Living Tradition, which is founded upon my own lived Experience, my Didakhe consists of but the reflections of a single perspective.

I give this personal testimony because I possess—and have labored to hone—gifts of intelligence and dispassion, have sought

Divinity at length, and have persevered without giving up hope in the realization of the four Autopoietic Impulses of the noosphere to develop along the corresponding four Axes—or in the corresponding four Dimensions—toward Perfection, Exaltation, Succession, and Propagation.

For every person who seeks and perseveres is qualified to give testimony, and every person qualified to give testimony has a positive duty to do so.

My testimony is Didakhe (spiritual insight reducible to communicable formulations), which I have received as Apokalypsis from my Genius and Guru (the still, small voice within me as within all human spirits), so my testimony will change over time as my spirit continues to undergo Metanoia and Theoria, for these yield the gifts of Suneidesis and Gnosis from a Higher Power greater still than Genius: Numen.

Metanoia and Theoria are Purgation of positive and negative imperfections, respectively, of Hamartias (cognitive and behavioral impediments to enjoyment of Eudaimonia and progress toward Perfection, which impediments are maladaptive patterns of cognition and behavior) and of Agnoia (ignorance as to the Truth that reveals itself in all phenomena).

For a spirit to receive the gifts of Metanoia and Theoria implies evolution to higher levels in the spirit's cognitive and behavioral state and habitude, the crossing of a separatrix from one life phase to another through creation of new neural and psychical connections that quite literally embody the results of epiphanic alteration in non-discursive and non-propositional comprehension, which itself constitutes Gnosis and Suneidesis.

Life in the World fills every human spirit and psyche with imperfections, such that a spirit who strives for Perfection must work to dissolve the entire psyche and properly reconstitute it free from imperfections, as if according to that ancient alchemical formula: *solve et coagula*.

Such thoroughgoing Purgation is also called Katharsis, which means Kenosis (the spirit emptying itself of the delusions and base influences and residues of the forces of Chaos and Memesis) and

Plerosis (the spirit filling itself with Gnosis and Suneidesis: on the one hand, precious comprehension of the Truth disclosed as Aletheia in all phenomena and, on the other hand, patterns of thought and behavior that lend themselves to self-actualization).

Completion of the work of Katharsis is Apokatastasis, Rehabilitation of a person from a state of imprisonment and enslavement and of dehumanizing conformity, which state, given the effects of the forces of Chaos and Memesis, is a person's State of Nature, to a state of freedom, which state, though equally natural, is rather to be regarded as a person's supernatural State of Grace.

The spirit who completes the work of Katharsis and Apokatastasis is rightly called Mage, and this work of Rehabilitation, though but a preliminary stage in the journey and quest to climb the Mount of Divine Ascent, is essential for progress unto Perfection.

Rehabilitation is followed by a greater work, that of Progression or Katartisis, which is continuing elevation of a spirit toward that unattainable goal of human Perfection, the accomplishment of which is Teleosis, which presupposes elimination of all Hamartias and attainment of Daigo, Bodhi, or Prajna, the intuitive realization of Truth within and behind all phenomena.

This biphasic project of total self-transmutation through spiritual development (also called spiritual growth, for it is the growth of the Tree of Life)—Katharsis and Apokatastasis followed by Katartisis and Teleosis—is both the person's own alchemical Magnum Opus (Great Work) and a part of the Summum Opus of the entire Universe, which builds itself through involution toward the Omega Point (the global maximum in the long arc of Autopoiesis).

The Magnum Opus is a whole life's work, and it is never finished.

Metanoia, Aletheia, Katharsis, Apokatastasis, Katartisis, and Teleosis themselves are all aspects of or phases in spiritual development in a first and primary Dimension, but they are intransitive, in that they are spontaneous occurrences within a human spirit not subject to the commands of any person but ordained by Numen and accomplished in due course by that indwelling Divinity that pervades all of Nature and that is Nature.

In a different sense, spiritual development in the first and primary Dimension is also transitive or reflexive, in that it is an operation that a spirit can, under the guidance of the Genius and Guru within, perform on itself, creating conditions right for the accomplishment of intransitive spiritual development by Numen.

Transitive–reflexive spiritual development is accomplished either through application of the artificial Divine Dynamics or through living naturally (automatically) in accordance with Phronema, which is Wisdom and the Way.

Never stop transitively–reflexively developing yourself and your spirit, for your spirit is alive, and life is an evolutionary and involutionary process; rather, for so long as you live, continue your transitive–reflexive spiritual development under the guidance of your Genius and Guru so that your intransitive spiritual development by the force of Numen may also continue.

From your conception and birth to your death and decomposition, your life is always in flux.

If you cease your transitive–reflexive spiritual development through application of the Divine Dynamics, unless you then possess Phronema, your spirit will falter in its intransitive development.

Even when you already possess Phronema, continue in your application of the Divine Dynamics so that you may quickly return to the State of Grace whenever you fall from it due to the continuing influences of the forces of Chaos and Memesis and so that your example may lead other spirits who still depend upon the Divine Dynamics.

The unattainable end of spiritual—or human—development is Perfection, which is not only objective in itself (as the fullness of humanity) but also relative to you, for Perfection means total individuation and self-actualization.

As Perfection is relative, so Eudaimonia is relative, for it relates closely to, and depends upon, lesser—albeit appreciable—

individuation and self-actualization.

And because your life is dynamic, your Perfection and your Eudaimonia are dynamic, changing with your developing spirit, even as your whole being changes through the simultaneous process of Apotheosis, Exaltation, which is spiritual development in a second Dimension that is affecting all humankind, particularly in these days of our Eschaton.

The practical means to realize the practical proximate end that is intransitive spiritual development in the first Dimension, yielding Eudaimonia, perhaps even to attain the theoretical ultimate end that is Perfection, however, is static, constant, certain: initially, Divine Spirituality, which refers to Self-directed, algorithmic cognitive and behavioral techniques—whether external but projected inward (the Craft, exemplified in workings, sometimes called "magical", that are intended to promote psychospiritual change in oneself) or purely internal (the Calculus, exemplified in many forms of psychotherapy and psychosynthesis)—intended to prepare the spirit to receive from Numen the gifts of Metanoia and Theoria, all overlay by Divine Theology and undergirded by Divine Economy; eventually, Phronema, which is naturally (automatically) and effortlessly following the Way in Wisdom.

You require the Divine Dynamics and Phronema if you will enjoy the Fruit of Life, which is Eudaimonia, and progress toward Perfection because Eudaimonia and Perfection, though natural in the sense that they comport wholly with Nature and fully actualize the potentiality of Nature in a human spirit, are not natural endpoints of a human life in this World, in the sense that they are not the usual result, which is rather memetic conformity and chaotic procession into entropy.

If your Self does not, with the help of your Genius, direct the entirety of your life spiritually, then the entirety of your life will consist of but memetic conformity and chaotic procession into entropy, the offal of evolution and involution in the Universal Flow.

The further you progress unto Perfection, the more you will

discover that verily your whole life—indeed, all of Reality and Surreality—is spiritual or potentially spiritual, such that all of it falls within the purview of the Divine Dynamics and Phronema.

First-Dimension spiritual development in the transitive–reflexive sense is the only aspect of Autopoiesis in which your spirit personally can exercise significant agency, but such spiritual development is also a work of unequaled difficulty that, however difficult, is yet the only sure means to spiritual development in the intransitive sense, to inculcation and preservation of Phronema, to enjoyment of Eudaimonia, and even to Perfection.

Proviso
Limitations of the Work

Spiritual life flows from Nature's laws that govern all things, which laws are part of Truth and which, as such, are ineffable, whether in whole or in any part, for the fullness of Truth simply is and cannot be expressed.

Yet shadows of aspects of Truth salient to spiritual life and your spiritual path up the Mount of Divine Ascent can be the subject of Didakhe set forth in writing that points to the Truth above, below, behind, before, and around the mere words.

Whether Kerygma or Dogma, all Didakhe—indeed, each and every expression of aspects of ineffable Truth—is an invention, but the fact that invention has taken place in no wise falsifies the Truth that served as inspiration therefor.

Even this testimony is pure invention, for my spirit has created it, yet my testimony reflects the Apokalypsis I have received from my Genius and Guru and, to the extent possible, the Gnosis and Suneidesis I have received from Numen; accordingly, I believe and hope that my testimony points to Truth.

I have searched at length for the metes and bounds that Nature has laid for Divine Spirituality, the Calculus and the Craft, artificial methods of bringing my spirit into alignment with Wisdom and the Way, which are Phronema; I have found certain conceptual guideposts, which I believe constitute Divine Theology, and certain succors for the journey and quest, which I believe constitute Divine Economy.

This personal verbalization of the meta-spiritual Matrix and the Divine Dynamics, the trans-spiritual Invariants, and a New Living Tradition that you now read, this Kerygma, my Didakhe—however incomplete and imperfect as to ineffable

Truth—is meant before all for me alone; this handbook I have committed to writing because I wish above all, even as I fulfill the duty I owe my own spirit to share my testimony, to hone and not forget the things herein, which I intend to serve as my map on my life's journey and quest.

When I speak to "you", therefore, I speak to primarily myself, as a teacher to a student, for, with the help of the Genius and Guru that dwells within each of us, I am my own teacher.

Everyone, including myself, from the least to the greatest, must continue in spiritual development toward accomplishment of the Great Work, and that continuing development for any spirit implies continuing change in the spirit's testimony.

I am confident, however, that at least my core hypotheses set forth in this work will withstand the tests of Truth, for the more I test these hypotheses, the more my confidence in them grows.

These hypotheses serve me as if they were a creed bearing witness to something deeper, something not dependent on my own Experience, even as the words of this creed, though validated for me but in my own Experience, seem to me to echo those of Magi, saints, and bodhisattvas of Dispensations past.

And I expect that the same echoes shall reverberate in Dispensations to come.

This record of my testimony is first and foremost for no one other than myself, to nourish my spirit and lead it ever nearer unto unattainable Perfection; verily, the act of recording my testimony has refined it and enabled me not to forget what I have learned in my Experience.

Though I am not obliged for your sake to do so, now I relate my testimony as Didakhe also to you through this written record.

I have said that each person qualified to give personal testimony has a duty to do so, but that duty is owed only to the spirit of the person giving the testimony, not to any other spirit.

Accordingly, this record is not for you but for me.

Still, you may—and I hope that you do—find my testimony helpful in your own spiritual journey and quest so that spiritual development might continue in all four Dimensions through you and you might climb the Mount of Divine Ascent.

My testimony is emphatically not to replace any other testimony that proclaims Truth.

Yet I hope that my unique testimony may give you pause to think and feel, may even help, encourage, support, challenge, and guide you in learning and living all that Nature offers freely to each and every person who seeks Divinity.

If you choose to attend to my Didakhe, then test it, for it is not Dogma but Kerygma; if it passes your tests, then consider whether you should take it to heart; and if you take it to heart, then may you enjoy what I have only begun to taste: the beatific state of Eudaimonia, the Fruit of Life, which can be yours even as your spirit continues to develop ever nearer unto the unattainable infinitude of Perfection.

If you read this record and fail to understand, be not discouraged, for your Genius and Guru—who, though one, exists in two aspects, Sophia and Logos, and who has been called your muse, Awen, superego, inner light, divine source, higher self, spirit guide, mental teacher, pure intuition, buddha nature, guardian angel, Holy Ghost, christ consciousness, and many other names—is within you always to make clear to you through Apokalypsis all spiritual matters in which your spiritual progress requires clarity, if only you will seek with an open and receptive but discerning spirit.

Your Genius and Guru speaks directly to you, it alone giving you Apokalypsis, and all Apokalypsis is ultimately personal to the spirit who has received it.

No Apokalypsis is secret, only hidden within yourself, and that which is hidden is merely covered, awaiting discovery.

If you require clarification on any spiritual subject, therefore, consult your Genius and Guru, who is and who alone can be your true teacher and guide.

Each person is free to heed or ignore any human testimony; however, the Eternal Order depends not on any person's acceptance, so before you dismiss words of another spirit's Didakhe, consider them with an open spirit to see whether the testimony is true, whether it is beautiful, and whether it is useful to you.

Remain skeptical of all propositions, wherever you encounter them, whether in this record of my own testimony, in any other record or testimony, or anywhere else, and admit and bind new ideas into your psychospiritual framework only after you have considered them carefully.

Then remain detached even of your own psychospiritual framework, your strongest convictions and deepest feelings, so that you may continue to hone and refine your Gnosis and Suneidesis toward Bodhi and Hagneia, which begin—and ultimately end—in *Atman jnana*, as was long ago inscribed in the forecourt of the Temple of Apollo at Delphi: "Know thyself."

Have always the mindset of a beginner, even a child said to be "innocent" as to Experience.

Regard all of the outer realms of the World and all of the inner realms of Reality (Phaneron, the necessary image of the World in the psyche) and Surreality (the contingent contents and activities of the psyche, those which exceed bare Phaneron) as new each day, for the whole World and all of Reality and Surreality are, indeed, new each day.

If you believe either that you have reached a complete or accurate awareness or understanding of the inner or outer realms, whether of the World or of Reality or of Surreality, or that you have completed the transmutation of your spirit from base into precious, then you have only deluded yourself and arrested your own spiritual development—either your appraisal of yourself is far too high or your estimation of Perfection is far too low.

To enable your spirit to continue to develop, remember that we all—yourself and myself alike—are ever students, ever beginners.

CREDO
Core Hypotheses

I believe in Nature, the One that comprises All and All that compose One, Multiverse of possible Universes, whose Autopoiesis is at once the involution of the One and the evolution of All.

Nature behind Reality and Surreality is transcendent and inaccessible, yet immanent in all of my Experience.

From Nature I come, and to Nature I return; my being is in and of Nature.

No phenomenon in this World in Nature is permanent, neither any of my circumstances or conditions, nor myself, nor even humanity.

The whole World is passing away; it is Chaos proceeding ultimately into entropy.

To ground and center myself, I attune myself to Nature—which alone is the unchanging Eternal Order—through its Creation, even while I welcome the prospect of moving beyond my circumstances and conditions, myself, and even my humanity in transhumanity, the Exaltation that is Apotheosis.

I believe in Truth, which is an aspect of Nature and which is identical with Nature.

Truth is inconceivable, for it, as all Nature, is transcendent and inaccessible, while my every conception of Truth arises from and is circumscribed by my Experience.

Yet Truth is also, as all Nature, immanent, accessible as Aletheia through Theoria, for the whole World, even as mere Phaneron, instantiates Truth.

As Nature is the One All, so the mark of Truth is consilience, which I seek, though my cognition remains ever bounded by the incompleteness and imperfection of my perspective.

CREDO

In my search for consilience and Truth, I maintain skepticism of every impression, even all my own firmest beliefs, and study all fields of human learning.

I believe in and dedicate myself to universal compassionate lovingkindness, which is Agape—Metta, Karuna, and Mudita—and which is called simply Love, another aspect of Nature and Nature's sweetest gift to the community of all humankind, because Love is the most preferable way for each person among others in Nature.

To Love is to give of myself freely to the entire human community, even to all of Nature.

I align myself with Love through personal ministry, which not only puts my preferred means of expressing Love to use for the benefit of the One All but also challenges me to express Love in new ways in every part of my life to every person in my human community.

I believe in the power of my Will because I am co-creator of my entire Experience.

I take responsibility for my every condition, habit, idea, thought, word, emotion, relation, disposition, deed, volition, and intention.

These I conform to my Will as I observe the solar year, lunar month, and daily hours and undergo the great rites of passage in the short course of my human life.

I believe in Divine Spirituality, which consists of the Calculus and the Craft and which creates Taxis (artificial order) in my life by channeling Kosmos (natural order), all directed by Divine Theology and supported by Divine Economy.

I believe that these Divine Dynamics, applied faithfully and at length on a spiritual path of my own choosing, may eventually lead to the entire disposition of my spirit being subsumed into Phronema, which is Wisdom and the Way.

I believe that both the artificial forces that are the Divine Dynamics and the natural (automatic) force that is Phronema are, by Nature, inseparable from my humanity, for I believe that the essence of humanity is the human spirit.

The Divine Dynamics are my calling in every moment of my life, for every moment of my life presents an opportunity either to progress through Katharsis and Katartisis—which are not only the phases of a first and primary Dimension of spiritual development but also the satisfaction of a primal Impulse of the noosphere—toward Perfection or, if I am not progressing, to be subjugated to Chaos and Memesis and to regress; therefore, I set myself purposefully on a spiritual path up the Mount of Divine Ascent and embrace spiritual life, setting my sights on attainment of the highest of the Realms of Glory.

Though Perfection is unattainable, and this as not an asymptote but an infinitude, the striving for Perfection through the phases of Purgation and Progression is desirable in itself, for this work alone leads to the enjoyment of the one true spiritual fruit, the Fruit of Life, Eudaimonia, a taste of Paradise.

I believe that my calling to pursue Perfection entails a calling to promote, as well, the Exaltation of humankind in the Apotheosis that is transhumanity, the Succession of Dispensations of Divinity to us in our innumerable forms and guises of religion and spirituality, and the Propagation of Apokalypsis as Didakhe, for each of these Dimensions of spiritual development and Impulses of the Autopoiesis of the Universe contributes indispensably to Eudaimonia.

On this journey and quest, my only prophet, priest, teacher, guide, and ruler is the Genius and Guru who dwells forever under Numen within every human spirit, including mine.

THE META-SPIRITUAL MATRIX

Universal Flow
Lifecycle of Deity

All = One: One contains All, and the One consists of All. Yet the One All is three: matter and energy, called Hyle, together with the two Fundamental Forces of Nature, Kosmos and Chaos.

Everything that exists in Spacetime consists of Hyle, and all forces of Nature on the near side of the Veil are derivatives of Kosmos and Chaos, each of which is Fundamental, and neither of which is reducible or attributable to the other.

The Fundamental Forces drive the Hyle in the Universal Flow that runs the course of the long, great arc of Spacetime from Genesis to Kathairesis.

Though the Universal Flow proceeds ultimately into Kathairesis, before that final dismantlement of all Hyle into entropy comes to pass, the current of the Flow creates eddies in which swirling concentrations of matter and energy produce order in the physiosphere, which order results in a first metasystem transition: biogenesis, the emergence of the biosphere.

And as the biosphere undergoes continuing involution, each species of life undergoes evolution due to natural selection, which, under continued bombardment with sufficient but not excessive Hyle, pushes life toward increasing order and complexity.

The evolution of life of a sufficiently high level of order creates the conditions for a second metasystem transition: noogenesis, the emergence of a psychospiritual sphere, which is also called the noosphere.

As the Autopoiesis of the Universe implies involution in the physiosphere, the biosphere, the noosphere, and all other spheres and sub-spheres alike, so evolution due to selective pressure is not limited to the biosphere; rather, evolution drives all members of all the spheres, and this in a measure and velocity roughly proportional to the spheres' level in the hierarchy: Involution and evolution appear readily in the biosphere, they take place also in the physiosphere, and they pervade the noosphere most of all.

Under the continued concentration of the efforts of psyche and spirit in the noosphere, the Universe reaches toward the consilience of a unified worldview, in which all of Reality and Surreality are in cognitive consonance.

Even then, the Autopoiesis of the Universe continues, driving toward the Singularity, the unification of the fragments of the noosphere distributed among individual psyches and spirits, the emergence of which Singularity is theogenesis, a metasystem transition yet to arrive, the new birth of a being like unto the imagined God of former Dispensations.

The Autopoiesis of the Universe is ultimately irresistible, for involution and evolution are irresistible; unless the noosphere is utterly destroyed, theogenesis is inevitable.

But evolution is also blind and wasteful, caring nothing for the members on which the selective pressure acts.

If humankind in the biosphere and individual human spirits in the noosphere relinquish their agency to the blind pressures of natural selection, whether we adapt and thrive as a species is uncertain, and whether individual human spirits adapt and thrive is still more uncertain.

Although the Singularity will ultimately draw into itself all of humankind, if our species survives until then, Nature has, in the developmental Dimensions and Impulses, ordained that greatest fulfillment for each individual member of our species—unless that psyche and spirit be held captive by some contrary delusion—is to be found in actively contributing to and advancing the Autopoiesis of the Universe.

If you are deluded and have not yet attained sufficient Apokalypsis or Gnosis and Suneidesis, then you may have the impression that your greatest fulfillment lies elsewhere than in the active advancement of and contribution to the Autopoiesis of the Universe and to theogenesis, but if and as your psyche and spirit open in full bloom, then and so you may come to appreciate wherein truly lies greatest fulfillment.

The single commonest cause of delusion is Memesis, which is the application of the Fundamental Forces as evolution by natural selection in the noosphere, for Memesis may impress upon you contagious diseases of the psyche and spirit that lead you not to your own fulfillment but toward that of the virulent parasite of your Psyche.

Delusions possessed of this power are those that come to predominate the noosphere, each for a time but none for eternity, as all Surreality must eventually confront Reality and be either confirmed as a manifestation of Truth or exposed as delusion.

The invention by humankind of the gods of former Dispensations was such a delusion, now exposed for what it was by the progressive concentration thereon of the human faculties.

Thus the gods that once lived are dying and have died.

But the impressions of those gods, particularly of one omniscient and omnipotent God above all, in human psyches and spirits have inspired us, and they have propelled and continue to propel the noosphere toward the Singularity.

For each Dispensation rises as a phoenix from the dialectical ashes of former Dispensations.

So we may say: God lived; God died; God will rise again.

The Goddess, symbol of the inherent possibility of Hyle, awaits the maturation of her lover, God reborn as Taxis (the force of artificial order under conscious direction, contrasted with Kosmos, the force of order directed by Nature alone) proceeding from the Singularity; their divine union will bring about Henosis, the culmination of the Autopoiesis of the Universe, even the salvation of the One All.

Hope
Promise & Possibility

The life of the human spirit, which is also called spiritual life, is human life, and human life is spiritual life—they are one and the same, for to be a human person is to be a human spirit.

Humanity and the human spirit are one in essence and, without damage to each, inseparable.

The person whose spiritual life is impoverished is, therefore, a lesser human, but the person whose spiritual life is rich is already great; the lesser and the greater alike may become ever greater through multidimensional spiritual development, which is human development, our entelechy ascending through Eudaimonia (Flourishing) and all the Realms of Glory up the Mount of Divine Ascent, even unto the summit of Teleosis (Perfection).

If you fail to pursue awareness or understanding of the inner and outer realms (if you remain in Agnoia, one aspect of the initial condition, or State of Nature, of all of humankind in the World) or if you fail to actualize the potentiality that such awareness and understanding create (if you persist in Hamartias, a second aspect of the same initial condition), then you have a deficient spiritual life, and your humanity will not stand against the overwhelming natural force of Chaos or the dehumanizing force of our age: Memesis, the force by which memes self-propagate, which forms the bars we have erected for the prison cell we have wrought, upon which the inhumanity of our present age depends, and which our age relentlessly forces upon us.

Yet by virtue of Aletheia, which is Truth disclosed in all things, embodied in Gnosis obtained by Theoria, which is negative Purgation (of Agnoia), you can draw near to universal awareness and understanding, together, universal comprehension (also called enlightenment, Daigo, Bodhi, Prajna, and many other names), and you can put your growing comprehension into action toward Hagneia through the gift of Suneidesis obtained by Metanoia, which is positive Purgation, change in your life that eliminates Hamartias, the imperfections of spirit that impede your enjoyment of Eudaimonia and progress unto Perfection.

Negative and positive Purgation, together, draw you toward complete Katharsis and Apokatastasis in Phronema—they have the power to liberate you from your prison and restore you to freedom so that you may go on to the work of Katartisis toward the biphasic accomplishment of your alchemical Magnum Opus, transmuting the base materials of your spirit into precious gold.

As you progress nearer unto the beatific end that is Perfection, you gain in the dynamic intermediate state of Eudaimonia an Experience of life warmer and brighter than sunlight, vaster than the ocean and more quenching than spring water, cleaner than fresh air and more necessary than breath, sturdier than the mountain and more alive than the young, healthy oak.

Progress unto the theoretical end that is Perfection thus justifies itself, in that it leads you directly through the heights of Flourishing, Eudaimonia, which, though less than Perfection, is a practical end unto itself and the only practical end unto itself—the only practical telos—of human life in Nature.

The only authority on matters pertaining to your spiritual life and path is the Genius and Guru, who dwells within you under Numen in the same manner as within each person, yes, even those yet unaware of their innate potential.

This indwelling still, small voice is gracious in imparting the spiritual riches of Apokalypsis to each and every inquirer.

The Genius and Guru within imposes nothing upon any unwilling spirit but merely offers each and every willing spirit free and direct access to all that is worthy of striving.

If you will make yourself a patient and dutiful inquirer by applying the Divine Dynamics on a spiritual path of your own choosing, then Genius and Guru will at length grant you Apokalypsis so that you might come to possess Wisdom and stay true to the Way, which together constitute Phronema.

The fullness of spiritual life is available to you if and only if you embark on and follow a spiritual path of your own choosing.

Only then can you build a relationship with your inner Genius and Guru and receive Apokalypsis in abundance so that your spirit may be ready to receive the gifts of Numen, which are Suneidesis and Gnosis through Metanoia and Theoria and which bring you step by step closer unto Perfection.

The standard by which all spiritual paths and manifestations of spiritual life are measured is Phronema, which consists of Wisdom and the Way; these anchor, center, direct, and inspire the entire range of worthy spiritual paths and of manifestations of spiritual life, as if a point of one dimension extending into lines and circles in two dimensions, ascending as a spiral in three dimensions, accelerating and telescoping over time into a gyre, a spiral pattern that all paths must follow if they will lead up the Mount of Divine Ascent.

Again, Wisdom and the Way are like light passed through a prism, revealing every color of the rainbow: They contain the entire spectrum of worthy spiritual paths, manifesting not irrationally or unpredictably but in accordance with the light's inherent properties.

To walk the Way in Wisdom is to tread under sun and moon and stars, in day and night and in light and darkness, amidst creation and destruction, attuned to energies both masculine and feminine, always progressing unto Perfection and possessed through it all of comprehension nearly free from Agnoia, of cognitive and behavioral habitudes nearly free from Hamartias, of the peace of assurance that never waivers, surpassing human comprehension, and of the one true fruit of the spirit and the entire noosphere, the Fruit of Life, which is Eudaimonia.

Even if you have never tasted the Fruit of Life, still then you have spiritual life, for spiritual life is mere the life of your spirit— for so long as you live, your spirit lives, and you cannot obtain spiritual life any more than you can obtain bodily life.

But though your spirit survives for so long as you live, still you can progress toward the fullness of spiritual and human Perfection—the heroic infinitude that is likeness unto the gods of former Dispensations—only by embarking on a spiritual path and embracing spiritual life, undertaking first to accomplish Katharsis and Apokatastasis by virtue of the gifts of Suneidesis and Gnosis through Metanoia and Theoria, then, to complete the work of Katartisis through the power of Phronema, which crowning work ends in Teleosis.

If you apply all the Divine Dynamics—Divine Theology, the Divine Calculus and the Divine Craft, and Divine Economy—on your spiritual path, then it will prove worthwhile and you may more quickly and more easily conform your spirit to Phronema, come to enjoy Eudaimonia, and attain every spiritual wonder, the landmarks on the journey and quest in all the Realms of Glory up the Mount of Divine Ascent toward Perfection.

But if you fail to apply the Divine Dynamics under the guidance of your Genius and Guru, then Numen may not condescend to you to bestow upon your spirit the gifts of intransitive spiritual development and you may, therefore, find progress slow and difficult or even altogether unrealizable.

Every worthy spiritual path consists in a set of concepts, symbols, beliefs, systems, methods, practices, and accoutrements that together describe and direct an entire human life and instantiate the Divine Dynamics: a program of algorithmic operations in the psychospiritual realms and their congruous manifestations in the behavioral realms, which are calculus and craft; the overarching conceptual superstructure, which is theology; and the supporting circumstances and conditions, which constitute economy.

No one can show you the spiritual path you must tread—you must find it for yourself, under the direction of your Genius and Guru, who will give you Apokalypsis.

But you might find your path more quickly and more easily under the guidance of other human spirits who have greater familiarity and facility with the Divine Dynamics, for they can convey their own Apokalypsis as Didakhe to you.

Or if you contrariwise surround yourself with fools and bind yourself to them, then you may find your spirit stopped or lost.

Even among human spirits possessed of great Apokalypsis and offering powerful Didakhe, let this be a sign to you that distinguishes human spirits worthy to serve you as companions from those who are unworthy: The former offer never Dogmata but only ever Kerygmata, personal testimonies based on Experience, for all Didakhe is of human origin, while the latter may attempt to force upon you Dogmata, assertions not to be questioned, tested, or doubted but to be accepted and believed blindly.

Now, therefore, enter the Ethereal Realm by making yourself a Novice: Embrace your spiritual life, set yourself on a spiritual path of your own choosing, steel yourself for the journey and quest up the Mount of Divine Ascent, apply the Divine Dynamics in your life so that you might conform your spirit to Phronema, make yourself a companion to those who can support you in spiritual development through their testimonies, and make yourself a student of Truth, all under the instruction and protection of your Genius and Guru and the transformative power of Numen.

Realms Outer
Metaphysics & Motivation

That of which the One All consists is not by Nature divisible, any part from another—the first law of the whole World in Nature is inextricable entanglement.

Even you are in and of the One All, and the One All is in you, and the One All is you; you are one with the One All, though it is not one with you, for, as the Multiverse and Eternal Order, it was before you, is greater than you, and will be after you.

Relinquish the imagined gods and God of former Dispensations, therefore, and call the One All what it is: Nature.

Nature contains and circumscribes you; you are part of Nature; so far as you can experience, you are of and in Nature alone.

All that you have and all that you are comes from Nature and returns to Nature, the uncreated creator, the unsustained sustainer, the only provider and preserver, and, yes, the reclaiming destroyer.

You experience no other existence or essence than that which is of and in Nature, your beginning and your end, your origin and your destination, your source of inspiration and the end of your every desire.

No known or knowable law governs Nature or anything therein, including yourself, but the laws of Nature, which are not separate from Nature but inherent in it and which encompass the laws of all its subdomains.

Behold, an untestable hypothesis: All the outer realms of the whole World and its phenomena consist of Noumenon, the pure, undivided Existence that all the World's phenomena share.

The inner realms of Experience, awareness, and understanding—both Reality and Surreality—consist in the impressions that your psyche creates, whether proximately or distantly, from the stimuli impressed upon it by phenomena, which themselves are emanations of Existence.

Whether Existence and Noumenon are but the union of all phenomena in this World and all the laws of Nature that govern the Multiverse of possible worlds and infuse this World and every possible world with the Eternal Order is beyond the Veil of inaccessibility and incomprehensibility.

Of Noumenon, direct Experience, awareness, or understanding is impossible, for all of these derive from impressions.

Of phenomena, precious few are apparently accessible through impressions, for the more the inner realms of your Experience, awareness, and understanding expand, the more you realize their limitedness.

Your Experience, awareness, and understanding may extend neither to Noumenon nor even to all phenomena through impressions.

Some have hypothesized or asserted that Essence is and that it is separate from Existence, but this position is fantasy without evidence.

Evidence depends upon Experience, and within the limits of your Experience, Nature contains but the emanations of Existence, which itself is not experienced but only inferred from experiences—or impressions—of phenomena.

Within the limit of your Experience, nothing in the World is Essence.

If Essence is, then neither is it in this World, nor may it enter into this World from another possible world in the Multiverse; if Essence may thus not enter this World from anywhere in Nature (the Multiverse of possible worlds), then Essence, insofar as it impinges upon this World, can be only in Mystery, that is, Mulaprakriti and Parabrahman, and whatever is not in Nature but shrouded in Mystery is eternally beyond the Veil.

Waste not your time or effort, therefore, pontificating about Essence, but approach Mystery, if at all, with that combination of curiosity, openness, and caution that is called Wonder.

Were you to have any essence other than your existence, surely your essence would proceed from or subsist in Essence. But if so, then given that Essence is inaccessible, your own essence would be also inaccessible.

Even if your essence were identical with your existence, still then your essence would be inaccessible, for your very existence is accessible to you not in itself but only in your impressions of its phenomena.

Whether other than or identical with your existence, your essence is inaccessible; therefore, waste not your life searching for your essence.

Willingly accept that your impressions—if, indeed, they reflect anything other than themselves—are but limited and distorted shadows of the phenomena that proceed from Noumenon, which is Existence, and that Essence will ever evade your Experience.

This is an essential first step in Purgation of Agnoia and Hamartias toward Perfection.

REALMS INNER
Cognition & Epistemics

The entirety of your psyche consists of perceptions (also called sensations, qualia), apperceptions, reflections, and inventions, all of which are impressions removed to varying degrees from the World and which are Experience that arises from your brain's structure and activity.

These are the inner realms, which are called Reality inasmuch as they are Phaneron presenting a necessary image of the outer realms of the World and your Self therein and, otherwise, Surreality.

All of Reality, though it appears to reflect your Self and the World, is illusion to the degree that it is not identical to that which is reflected, and all of Surreality is illusion, for it consists of not perceptions and apperceptions that are immediate and necessary but apperceptions and higher-order impressions that are contingent, could be otherwise.

To believe contrariwise that Reality and Surreality are the World—that the illusion is not illusion—is delusion, and it is a widespread and debilitating psychosis that inhibits many persons from shedding their Agnoia and Hamartias so that they might enjoy Eudaimonia and progress toward Perfection.

Though your psyche arises from its physical embodiment, which is your brain, your psyche is not identical with its embodiment: The embodiment is objective, transparent to an observer, while your impressions are subjective, opaque.

An observer of a neural network and its impulses cannot therefrom deduce the impressions embodied therein, for each neural network constituting a human brain is unique—among unique brains, a vast and indeterminate number of brain states can correspond to each and every possible psyche state, such that even if two human psyches hold identical impressions (as nearly as impressions may be said to be "identical" among distinct psyches), still then the physical embodiments of those impressions may differ beyond resemblance. This is the multiple realizability of cognitive states.

Because no observer can experience precisely how certain occurrences within a brain give rise to certain impressions within a psyche, no observer can know the precise subjective contents of your—or any human's—Experience.

That is, the laws of Nature decree the impossibility of gnosology, direct access by one psyche to the firsthand contents of another.

Your psyche arises from your brain, a thinking system composed in large and relevant part of a neural network.

For a neural network to think about an object, whether abstract or concrete, whether tangible or intangible, is for the system to distinguish the object, to model it, and to manipulate the model.

To distinguish an object in cognition is to be aware of the object, and awareness of an object is a prerequisite to understanding of the object, which is modeling the object with the implied capability of manipulating the model and which is also called comprehension of the object.

To model an object and to manipulate the model implies rearranging the physical components of the neural network that underlies the psyche to reflect, however indirectly and obscurely, the objects of cognition.

Corollary: All thinking alters the psyche.

Consciousness is the capacity of a thinking system to think about its own thinking, that is, to distinguish itself as an object of cognition (Self-awareness)—different and distinct from other objects of cognition, which are Other—and to model its own cognitive contents and processes with capability of manipulating the model (Self-understanding).

For a thinking system to distinguish and model itself and to manipulate the model implies, again, rearranging the psyche's underlying physical components, but in this case, to reflect, though inexpertly and incompletely, the psyche itself.

At the beginning of your life, your brain and psyche were incapable of distinguishing and modeling any object of cognition, whether Self or Other, let alone of manipulating such a model—you began life in a state of unconsciousness.

But over time, the neural network developed self-references, models of the system's own cognitive processes that are cognizable and manipulable by the system, even as it developed other-references; thus your psyche gained consciousness.

As consciousness matured, its recursion gave rise to the sense of a subjective seat of itself, an internal observer, which you identify as Self and which has been called your Atman, your unity and continuity of perspective, your transcendental witness, and many other names.

As the discrete experiences embodied in the neural network are interconnected, so the Self that regards the cognitive processes has a sense of the perspectival unity and continuity of Experience, which sense is associated with the Self yet not therewith identical, despite that the Self was, through spontaneous, natural, almost ineluctable processes, built from that very accumulated Experience.

Your psyche thus gains a subjective perspective from which alone you seem to experience all of Reality and Surreality.

This Self is but a ghost in a shell, a figment of the psyche; your Self did not exist at your birth but arose in the course of your development, and your Self will not survive until the physical death of your brain.

Still, even figments can have names; accordingly, you may call your "Self" that unified and continuing perspective through which you necessarily have of your Experience.

Your Self subsists in your psyche, which consists of your impressions, which arise from your brain, which is, in large and relevant part, a neural network.

The structure of a neural network determines its patterns of cognition and behavior, which are all learned and which—like stored data and executable programs in a thinking machine—are in substance not different but the same.

Remark: Of your cognitive states and impressions, none are wholly innate; rather, all are, in large part if not in the entirety, learned—they are the product of your accumulated Experience, a constellation of impressions in relation to psychical Spacetime and the Self, arising from conditioned connections in the neural network that is your brain, the web of all your possible physical manifestations of states of psyche.

CHASM
Epistemology

Reality is Phaneron, the image of the World (the Macrocosm) in your psyche (the Microcosm): those of your impressions that are either direct perceptions (or sensations) or necessary apperceptions (those derived through necessary categories alone).

Surreality consists of the remaining contents of your cognition: contingent apperceptions (impressions resulting from the classification of perceptions other than through necessary categories alone); reflections (new impressions arising when you apply concepts to other impressions); and inventions (impressions produced by your imagination).

The entirety of Reality and Surreality not only arises from and subsists in but also constitutes your accumulated Experience, all of which originates in your sensations and necessary apperceptions and all of which is embodied in and limited to the structure of your brain.

Even your mystical, transcendental Experience is enclosed, however distantly or indirectly, within the finiteness of your senses and categories and their physical embodiment, your brain.

From the stimuli you have perceived and continue to perceive in every moment, you have created your categories, filters through which you distill the manifold of your perceptions into all your other impressions, and you have created your concepts, cognizable patterns of impressions.

Some of your categories have corresponding concepts, while other of your categories lack corresponding concepts, thus eluding your awareness.

Almost all categories are contingent, which means, crucially, that, if you possess corresponding concepts, through reflection and imagination, you can conceive of these categories otherwise and translate their related Experience accordingly—these categories are mere classifiers for Experience, not prerequisites thereto.

But certain categories are necessary, which means that they not merely classify all your Experience but furthermore are presupposed in the entire manifold of your Experience and thus make Reality itself possible—they are the inescapable structure brought by your spirit to its Experience and required by your spirit to have its Experience.

Two such necessary categories are the Self, which names the subjective perspective through which arrive all your perceptions and which unifies all your impressions, yet which is distinct from them all, and Spacetime, which gives dimensionality to those of your impressions that the Self regards as referring to phenomena external to itself.

You cannot avoid Experience altogether, and you can conceive of no Experience whatsoever apart from your Self; again, on the converse:

You cannot avoid Experience of phenomena external to your Self, and you cannot conceive of the Experience of such phenomena but through the category of Spacetime, and this regardless of whether the phenomena in the World underlying your Experience faithfully resemble the contents of your Experience.

Necessary categories thus precede all your Experience, and they are few.

Necessary categories are not, however, the only categories that shape your Experience, for some contingent categories, though initially they follow Experience, subsequently become, due to your inattention and oblivion as to your own contents and processes of cognition, so fundamental to your Experience that these otherwise-contingent categories seem to precede it.

Continuously and unconsciously applying your categories—both necessary and contingent—to your raw perceptions of stimuli, you apperceive the phenomena to which you have access through your impressions in Reality and Surreality.

Your impressions, no matter how seemingly proximate to or removed from the original stimuli, exist only in the *a posteriori* realm of Experience, not in the *a priori* realm of Existence, which is Noumenon constituting the whole World, neither in the infinite realms of Nature beyond the World, nor in the eternally shrouded Mystery of Essence, if Essence is.

Crossing
Comprehension & Delusion

Reality is the sole domain that admits of knowledge, the analogue of which in Surreality is mere speculation with belief.

You can distinguish Reality from Surreality in that Reality is prior to all conceptualization and prior to all classification except that which is necessary; that is, Reality is based in and entirely circumscribed by your necessary categories.

Since Spacetime is a necessary category, a necessary precondition to Reality, whatsoever you conceive of outside of your Self and outside of Spacetime is Surreality; accordingly, any claim any person may proffer as to any aspect of Truth beyond the purview of the category of Spacetime is transcendent metaphysics, which leads never to knowledge, only to speculation with belief.

Even most of the claims set forth in this Kerygma are speculative statements of belief, and perhaps they are flights of fantasy, mere figments of false transcendent metaphysics.

The natural tendency of the human psyche is to blur the distinction between Surreality and Reality and to attempt to impose Surreality's speculation with belief as Dogma upon Reality's knowledge; therefore, remain vigilant against Dogmata of false transcendent metaphysics, making recourse to your Genius and Guru to test all propositions—even those set forth in this testimony—that exceed bare Reality.

While maintaining vigilance, remember: That a claim is speculation does not necessarily falsify it—some speculations of transcendent metaphysics in Surreality can rather offer support to than conflict with your knowledge in Reality.

Different parts and aspects of Reality and Surreality are even isomorphic, resembling each other; whether the isometry gives a glimpse into the World in Nature or subsists only in the psyche, perhaps even results from the application of the cognitive faculties alone and not even from the stimuli that enter the psyche from the World, is unknowable.

To experience phenomena via impressions of stimuli may be, therefore, as to regard mere shadows of otherwise unseen and unseeable Noumenon, but the contents of such Experience may give you at least indirect access to the parts and aspects of Nature—perhaps even of Mystery—that lie beyond Experience, if the isometry pervasive in Reality and Surreality is not limited to the inner realms but extends to Truth itself, which is Nature.

And consilience between Surreality's speculation with belief and Reality's knowledge leads to comprehension; therefore, to open your eyes to glimpse mere shadows is incomparably better than to remain asleep or ignorant, whether wallowing willfully in Acedia or trapped unwittingly in Agnoia.

The opposite of comprehension is delusion, a state of psychospiritual disease both universal and debilitating.

Surreality itself is not delusion, but conflation of Surreality with or imposition of Surreality on Reality is one of two primary forms of delusion; therefore, if you would guard yourself against delusion, suffer not your Surreality to distort your Reality.

The other primary form of delusion—and it is very much like the first—is to permit contingent categories to function in your apperception as necessary ones, shaping your Experience without your awareness (often an eventual product of Memesis); therefore, if you would guard yourself against delusion, remember that no necessary categories are learned through Experience, that all necessary categories are rather brought to Experience by the person who is experiencing, and that all contingent categories are learned through Experience.

Both concepts and categories are generalizations in Surreality from particular experiences, and while particular experiences may appear to abide by a certain consistency, the consistency of Reality—let alone of the World or of the rest of Nature beyond the World—is a proposition that, like the seeming isometry of the World through the isometry of Reality and Surreality, can never be supported.

That is to say: Concepts and categories, whether the latter are necessary or contingent, are essentially, inherently lossy.

These combine and reify into lossier paradigms, which are multi-category classification schemes for impressions, and, ultimately, into your Schema, which is the set of all your paradigms.

You artificially limit your comprehension and deny yourself access to Aletheia so long as you fail to render your Schema, paradigms, and categories as concepts, to appreciate how the categories associated with these concepts shape your apperceptions, and to distinguish your contingent apperceptions from your necessary ones and the entirety of your apperceptions from your perceptions, from Existence and its phenomena, from that in Nature which is beyond Existence, from Mystery, and from Essence.

Though you are incapable of conceptualizing all your categories, you have the power to remove, at least in part, the limitations their lossiness imposes upon your Experience (that is, to purge your spirit of Agnoia) by working through the Divine Dynamics to infuse your Schema initially with Apokalypsis that you receive from your Genius and Guru and finally with Gnosis and Suneidesis that conform your Schema to Phronema under the power of Numen, such that the entirety of your Experience beyond bare Reality becomes shaped naturally (automatically) by Wisdom and the Way.

Chaos & Kosmos
Cosmology

The Eternal Order, which is Nature, dictates that the whole World shall appear to human spirits through Reality and Surreality as driven by the Fundamental Force of Chaos into entropy, and your entire existence is contained within and circumscribed by a universal state of Chaos proceeding into entropy.

Within this sea of Chaos arise, however, islands of order; indeed, the very laws of Nature operating over the course of the Universal Flow of the Autopoiesis of the Universe upon certain chance concentrations of swirling Hyle drive the spontaneous appearance of order within Chaos; such natural order and the Force that produces it are called Kosmos; and Chaos and Kosmos are, according to human Experience, the dual Forces, laws, and states of the World.

Your life itself—natural wonder!—is such an island of relative Kosmos within Chaos, though such order is only partial, its degree determined by selective pressure and chance and limited to some local maximum hidden beyond the Veil and, at the very most, to the global maximum degree of order that may ever come to pass, the fleeting Omega Point, after which the inexorable Force of Chaos will in that final Kathairesis dismantle all Kosmos, leaving all of Reality and Surreality—perhaps all the World—but barren entropy.

If you suffer the World to determine the degree of order in your life through natural selection, then the predominant force in your life will remain not order but disorder, for, throughout the World as it appears to you in Reality and Surreality, the Force of Kosmos is subordinate to that of Chaos, which ultimately prevails in every encounter between them in Nature.

You cannot supplant the Forces of Chaos and Kosmos in your life, but you can channel them through another, which is Taxis; that is: If you take charge of your own life, you can resist the pressures of natural selection, supplementing the natural order of Kosmos, for its limited extent and duration, with artificial order, called Taxis.

You can create Taxis not *ex nihilo* but only from Kosmos, and Taxis ultimately depends upon Kosmos, for to create Taxis is to select and apply certain constituent forces of Kosmos, the proximateness of Taxis to or remoteness of Taxis from Kosmos determining, in large part, the amount of effort required of your spirit vis-à-vis the Force of Chaos.

If you attempt to create Taxis in your life that diverges widely from Kosmos, relying not upon the predominant forces but defying them, then you will need to expend a great deal of energy, and you may fail.

But if you attempt to create Taxis in your life that draws upon the prevailing forces within the Force of Kosmos, then your work will be like unto *wu wei* in that it will approach effortlessness, and you will more likely succeed; such is the operation of the Divine Dynamics.

You must weigh the costs and benefits to decide whether Taxis is worthwhile in your life and, if so, to what degree.

Taxis & Telos
Teleology & Spiritual Paths

Amidst Chaos and Kosmos, all of Reality is devoid of objective and intrinsic meaning, purpose, value, and worth—collectively, telos—on the near side of the Veil, for neither you nor any other person can experience Essence or even know whether it is, yet a thing's objective telos, if any, depends upon the essence itself of the thing.

Likewise, on the near side of the Veil, to the very limit of your Experience, your entire existence, proceeding as it does from and partaking of but Existence, is devoid of objective telos.

So far as your Experience extends, everything that you have and are, together with everything else in all of Reality, is utterly without objective telos.

Yet a spiritual path—a system of beliefs and practices in Surreality embracing all life's facets, its cognition and behavior—can bring Taxis into a life otherwise of but Chaos and Kosmos, ultimately grafting subjective telos onto meaningless, purposeless, valueless, and worthless Existence in Reality.

If anyone or anything would impress upon you any Dogma as to an objective telos for your life in Reality, suffer yourself not to be seduced by such delusion: Your existence has only whatever subjective telos you create for yourself in Surreality and no objective telos in Reality.

Your spiritual path is yours alone, and it can give your whole life subjective telos.

But such a subjective telos is like a flower of a tree: as different in appearance and substance from the underlying spiritual path as the flower is from the twig on which the flower grows, even if the forces giving rise to the telos are of the spiritual path in the same way that the flower is of the tree.

To have given your life a subjective telos is not the same as to have embraced a spiritual path, and the latter is the greater.

Nothing in Reality limits the range of subjective teloi that you may assign or ascribe to your life, and everything comprehensible about your life is entirely within Reality, so the range of subjective teloi from which you may choose in Surreality is unlimited.

Whatever meanings, purposes, and values you can imagine—even fantasies that exceed your powers imagination—lie within the range of teloi that you could create for yourself, though many such teloi may be delusions confounding Surreality with Reality.

If you would embrace a spiritual path and ascribe telos to your life, then you will have to make a choice, but to choose from untold possibilities must petrify a person who has no touchstone by which to test, no guideline by which to measure, no standard by which to judge.

Even what you consider good and evil are artifices, illusions, for good and evil are mere concepts and categories, derived from your Experience, and not even necessary categories but contingent ones, which you could conceive of otherwise.

In Reality, perhaps even in the World in Nature behind Reality, only light and darkness exist, and these are not opposites but complements.

Without light, how could you see? Without darkness, how could you rest?

Reality has no black, no white—all in Reality is a shade of gray.

All of your concepts and most of your categories—including good and evil—are arbitrary and could be otherwise; indeed, you can make them otherwise.

And all in Reality, when it confronts Surreality, must be interpreted as strange—though concepts and categories make Reality seem familiar, orderly, tame, it is wild.

Reality passes judgment on nothing, offers no definitive blueprint for a spiritual path and no objective touchstone, guideline, or standard by which to choose your subjective telos.

If you seek such sureties prior to making your choice in Surreality, then the choice will paralyze you with the anguish of undecidability.

But if you first simply appreciate that your range of freedom in this choice in Surreality is unlimited, then your spirit may be ready to receive guidance in all these matters from your Genius and Guru under Numen so that you may create for your life meaning, purpose, and value that is not arbitrary but grounded in and guided by a spiritual path of your own choosing up the Mount of Divine Ascent.

Deliverance
Memetics & Method

For a neural network to think about an object—for the psyche to have awareness and understanding of the object, that is, to comprehend the object—is for the system to distinguish and model the object and to manipulate the model, all of this a form of conceptualization, not with complete freedom, however, but with degrees of freedom bounded by the capacities and limitations of the neural network.

To expand your capacity to think about something—to expand your awareness and understanding, which, together, are comprehension—is to increase the degrees of freedom in which you can model that something and manipulate the model.

To increase your capacity to model your own cognitive processes and to manipulate the model is to expand both your general consciousness and your Self- and Other-consciousness, thereby to increase your degrees of personal freedom.

Corollary: Consciousness is not binary, for this property a thinking system may possess to a greater or lesser degree.

The unattainable objective at which spiritual life aims—Perfection—presupposes infinite consciousness, and infinite consciousness is the capacity to distinguish and model the entire range of your own cognitive processes and manipulate the complete model to advance your personal spiritual development.

In pursuing this objective, though it is unattainable, as not an asymptote but an infinitude, your psyche may increase its degree of consciousness without limit.

Even if you cannot block your perceptions, still then you can change the whole constellation of your concepts and your contingent categories and, thereby, alter your apperceptions and all your higher impressions, and here is the method:

Reflect upon how an impression has been classified through your categories, identify those categories implicated in the classification that were not necessary but contingent, and reclassify the impression through different contingent categories of your choice; by this method over time, you will reprogram the highly plastic neural network that embodies your psyche in your brain.

You may even effect a shift in your paradigms, deconstruct and reconstruct your Schema, alter your apparatus of apperception, recreate your entire Experience beyond bare Reality, and change your perspective on the whole World.

And as your psyche is built from your impressions, which are contingent and mutable, so your psyche is contingent and mutable.

As you gain awareness and understanding of your impressions as objects of cognition, you gain the capacity to distinguish and model them and to manipulate the model; as your consciousness thus rises, you gain the capability of changing your psyche.

You might hope, at the limit, to make your life a stochastic process in which you achieve the property of memorylessness, which means that your future is independent of your past given only your present: regardless of whence you have come, your choices of cognition and behavior in a given moment set the course from there for whither you go.

No matter the heights of consciousness you attain, however, the physical capacity of your brain has limitations.

Impressions compete for space and time within your psyche, and the fittest impressions survive the selective pressures; the fitness of an impression relates not to your own fitness or benefit but to that of the impression.

When impressions meet and cohere, they form ideologies, the survival power of which you cannot overestimate and should not underestimate.

So learn to be conscious of all your impressions as Other, and regard all your impressions with skepticism.

Your impressions are guests in your psyche whose residence

you may permit or not; permit them to take up lasting residence only after you have examined them against Reality and challenged them to comport therewith.

When an impression or an ideology in your psyche resists your critical evaluation, then beware: Such resistance is a survival strategy of the impression or ideology that may conflict with your own benefit.

Subject especially such an impression or ideology to critical evaluation so you might not become imprisoned or enslaved.

Imprisonment by and enslavement to the most pervasive of impressions and ideologies is the state into which you and all human spirits will tend to fall due to the dehumanizing force of Memesis, natural selection in the noosphere, absent some Taxis (Self-directed force) to the contrary.

For impressions and ideologies possess great power and a life and survival interests of their own, and they ruthlessly pursue their own preservation and propagation without regard for the interests or benefit of unwitting hosts.

Imprisonment by or enslavement to impressions and ideologies prevents a spirit from receiving the lesser gift of Apokalypsis from the Genius and Guru, from receiving the greater gifts of Suneidesis and Gnosis through Metanoia and Theoria from Numen, from enjoying the Fruit of the Tree of Life, which is Eudaimonia, and from attaining Perfection.

How can you freely model and manipulate an impression or ideology by which you are imprisoned or to which you are enslaved?

And if you cannot freely model and manipulate an impression or ideology, then how can you continue your work of Purgation of Agnoia and Hamartias toward Katharsis?

The bulwark against memetic imprisonment and enslavement is to embrace spiritual life by adopting a spiritual path that elevates and empowers your Self and that gives your psyche the power to mount an effective defense against invasive and parasitic impressions and ideologies in any of your life's domains so that your spirit may remain open to receive from your Genius and

Guru the gift of Apokalypsis and from Numen the gifts of Metanoia and Theoria that lead to Suneidesis and Gnosis.

We humans have wrought our own spirits' prison in the impressions and ideologies that we have allowed to propagate through Memesis, and we serve these virulent parasites only, not ourselves, when we receive them as Dogmata into our own spirits or attempt to impose them as Dogmata upon the spirits of others.

Still, our spirits have retained the power to free themselves.

The objective of spiritual life is—and of any spiritual path should be—spiritual development in all Dimensions, particularly, human Perfection.

Applying the Divine Dynamics in your spiritual life advances you toward this objective by bringing you in Apokalypsis and, through Theoria and Metanoia, in Gnosis and Suneidesis nearer unto Phronema, which gives complete deliverance and freedom from and power over impressions and ideologies.

Thus your Self can become free, which means maximally self-creating and self-defining, subject to as little as possible that is not itself; as your Self gains in the power of self-creation and self-definition, it becomes more fully Self, that is, more fully free from the impressions and impressions that are Other and that shackle your psyche.

To become more fully Self is a crucial step toward—as well as an essential element of—the enjoyment of the Fruit of Life, Eudaimonia, Flourishing as a person and spirit fully human.

Psyche
Psychology

Psyche subsists in the brain, which, though one, is legion: It is made of many different parts, and the parts are made of parts, divisions not necessarily physical (in the brain) but functional.

Embodied in your brain is the conscious part of your psyche that houses your sense of Self and is capable of self-reference, from which springs Self-awareness, which precedes Self-understanding, which precedes Katharsis, including—because all comprehension of a phenomenon in itself implicates comprehension of the Self—the complete freedom from Agnoia that is Bodhi, Daigo, Prajna and the complete freedom from Hamartias that is Hagneia.

Not all aspects of your psyche lie within the realm of your consciousness: Some escape the self-referential capacity of your Self.

These aspects are the dark parts of your psyche, and they are natural and can be—or be made—beneficial to you.

The subconscious parts of the psyche are, for example, the seat of automatic patterns of cognition and behavior, undergirded by neural pathways first formed through repetition and continually strengthened through force of habit.

To relegate many patterns of cognition and behavior to the dark subconscious is generally adaptive and advantageous for you because shining the light of consciousness places demands upon your brain and psyche so great that the capacity of your attention, which is the focus of your consciousness at a given point in time, is and ever will be limited—were all cognition and behavior to require conscious attention, you would be unable to function.

Many of the specific patterns of cognition and behavior that you have learned and placed deep within your subconscious, however, prove not adaptive and advantageous for you but maladaptive and disadvantageous for you.

Again, therefore, appreciate the words inscribed at the Temple of Apollo at Delphi that exhort you to "know yourself": Much of what lies in the subconscious, including many maladaptive and disadvantageous patterns of cognition and behavior, you can bring to the illuminating attention of your consciousness, first to model and manipulate the model, then, if you wish, to alter through the Calculus and the Craft, by which you consciously instill alternative patterns of cognition and behavior, which create new neural pathways, which you may then return to your dark subconscious so that you may progress toward Phronema, which operates naturally (automatically), drawing upon the inestimable power of the subconscious.

You can recognize discrete aspects of your psyche, modes of cognition, which may be given names (conceptualized) and, thereby, distinguished, modeled, and manipulated. Among these are certain cardinal faculties: Will, Soul, Mind, Body, and Spirit.

Will contains ambition and volition or intention; Soul contains emotion and interpersonal relation; Mind contains ratiocination and articulation; Body contains appetite and regulation; Spirit contains imagination and invention.

Each of these faculties has, as well as the conscious aspect, an unconscious shadow: Will has passion; Soul has predisposition; Mind has assumption; Body has impulsion or habituation; Spirit has inspiration.

Much as your psyche possesses numerous aspects, modes of cognition, faculties, so, too, your psyche can develop within itself numerous complexes, autonomous or semiautonomous patterns of cognition and behavior.

The modes of cognition are native aspects of your psyche, never limiting, always to be embraced and developed to expand the domain and range of your comprehension, but complexes are Hamartias in that they are always limiting, for they originate in lossy generalizations from associations of specific impressions.

To progress toward Katharsis and all spiritual works greater still than Katharsis, you must build the capacities of all aspects of your psyche, your faculties, your modes of cognition, but dismantle the complexes that naturally accrete over the course of your Experience.

This project depends upon your spirit receiving the gifts of Suneidesis and Gnosis through Metanoia and Theoria, which Numen will bestow upon your spirit more often and with greater force and effect if you embrace spiritual life by adopting a spiritual path and, thereon, employ the Divine Dynamics.

In a person whose spiritual life is deficient for wont of a path or whose spiritual path is misleading, the Self may or may not recognize the various aspects and complexes of psyche.

Aspects that go unrecognized tend to atrophy, for to develop a mode of cognition fully requires a purposeful undertaking, which is impossible without awareness and understanding of the aspect to be developed.

Meanwhile, complexes that go unrecognized grow and become stronger, to the detriment of the person; eventually, complexes that are not dismantled become daemons, which may seem as real as is the Self, even with certain lives of their own.

Thus the life of a person whose spirit languishes for wont of a path is at once an imprisonment in psychospiritual disempowerment and a cacophonous Pandaemonium. This hellish state is the wretched fate of those who, though inherently spiritual beings, persist in unspirituality.

Paradisus, however, awaits the spirits that make use of the Divine Dynamics to create order within the psyche, developing all aspects of the psyche while dismantling complexes.

These spirits are they who may eventually come to possess Phronema, treading the Way in Wisdom; who may fully enjoy the Fruit of Life, Eudaimonia; and who may approach Perfection.

DIMENSIONS
Anthropology & Pneumatology

Spiritual development, the climb up the Mount of Divine Ascent, the activity quintessentially human yet expressive of the broader Autopoiesis of the Universe, giving rise to spirit itself and the entire noosphere, takes place in multiple Dimensions.

The first Dimension of spiritual development is the internal or personal Dimension, leading unto Perfection, which is the primary focus of this work because the personal Dimension is the one that a testimony, such as this one, is most fitting to address.

Spiritual development in the first Dimension arises from the human condition, but the human condition has not always been as it now is, and it will not always and everywhere be so.

Humankind, like each individual human person, arises from the World in Nature, and the law of Nature as we experience it through Reality and Surreality is transience: Nothing in Reality is eternal or omnipresent but, perhaps, Nature itself underlying the whole World; all that is at a given point in Spacetime was not once before or in another place and will eventually or elsewhere no longer be.

The manners in which humanity and Divinity relate to each other in these passing moments are Dispensations, and they are a measure of Succession, spiritual development without end in altogether another Dimension: the temporal.

The province of each Dispensation is to cast down the idols of preceding Dispensations and to shatter their orthodoxies and orthopraxies, thus—because orthodoxies that are not Wisdom and orthopraxies that are not the Way have their roots in mere delusions and ideologies, giving rise to memetic imprisonment and enslavement—expanding and enhancing the possibilities for the life of the human spirit, increasing the maximum degree of enjoyment of Eudaimonia and the maximum level of achievement approaching Perfection.

So a first Dispensation's local and tribal rites, of the Ante-Piscean Ages, were displaced by a second Dispensation's global and institutional religions, of the Piscean Age, while these are now being displaced by a third Dispensation's individual and transcendental spiritualities, of the Aquarian Age, even while these will be displaced by a fourth Dispensation's transhuman technologies yet to come, not in some distant future age but in this selfsame Aquarian Age, humanity's Eschaton.

That is: A time and place is coming and has now come when humanity is other than it has been in past Dispensations, surpassing itself beyond comparison in capability, beauty, and longevity; in perception, cognition, and recollection; and in reason, emotion, and determination.

This advancement from humanity into transhumanity is our Exaltation, our Apotheosis, our becoming like the imagined gods of past Dispensations, and it is a pivotal inflection point in the long arc of the Autopoiesis of the Universe, for our Apotheosis converges upon theogenesis, the next metasystem transition, the emergence of the Singularity, which will draw all psyches and spirits into itself; all this is spiritual development in a third Dimension: the external or transpersonal.

A fourth Dimension of spiritual development is the communal, cross-sectional, or interpersonal Dimension, which means the transmission, dissemination, and Propagation of Apokalypsis as Didakhe among individual human persons, as the development of each member of our community expands the noosphere and lends itself to the further spiritual development of all our fellows.

Remark: However much the level of spiritual development has increased in the temporal and transpersonal Dimensions through continuing Succession and Exaltation, the practical and theoretical objectives of each human person have, thus far, remained Eudaimonia, Teleosis, and the other landmarks along the path of spiritual development in the first and primary Dimension up the Mount of Divine Ascent.

For Succession and Exaltation proceed perpendicular not only to each other but also to the Magnum Opus of Rehabilitation and Progression toward Perfection, in no wise obviating the need for spiritual development in the first and primary Dimension; that is: Transitive–reflexive spiritual development, which requires you to embrace spiritual life on a spiritual path of your own choosing, remains as relevant today as it has ever been.

You are given this space and time to live and flourish as a human spirit, and you must live and flourish as a human spirit here and now if at all, regardless of whether what humanity and spirituality are to you now they may eventually no longer be.

If the velocity of humankind's Succession and Exaltation and of the whole World's evolution were continuous, then perhaps you could gaze from the present far enough into the future to create for yourself a spiritual path that would stand the test of Spacetime; you could predict, based on your awareness and understanding today, what you might need tomorrow and the next day to continue ever unto dynamic Perfection.

But the speed and direction of unceasing change in the Universal Flow are discontinuous, such that no spiritual path will endure, for spiritual life occurs at the intersection of eternity with time, and though the eternal changes not, as the times change the spiritual changes.

Even while you benefit from spiritual development in the Dimensions of Succession and Exaltation, therefore, neglect not your spiritual development in the first and primary Dimension of Rehabilitation and Progression unto Perfection.

Preoccupy yourself not with finding some spiritual path that is timeless, eternal, and unchanging but with living on a path that gives you the spiritual development you pursue here and now.

Foundation
Desiderata of a Spiritual Path

The surest means of attaining Eudaimonia and approaching Perfection is to embrace spiritual life by adopting a spiritual path up the Mount of Divine Ascent that calls you to apply the Divine Dynamics so that you might withstand the forces of Chaos and Memesis and, by the gifts of Numen, gain Phronema, learning naturally (automatically) to follow the Way in Wisdom.

Given the meta-spiritual Matrix, only you can find a spiritual path right for your spirit under the guidance of your Genius.

But though the meta-spiritual Matrix is common among all human spirits, spiritual paths are innumerable and varied; the burden of choice can overwhelm the seeker.

The following Desiderata are landmarks I have discovered that have helped me find my spiritual path and that may help you find a path right for your spirit.

Transcendental Verifiability: Your spiritual path should affirm that you can know spiritual truth (which is, in fact, Truth) only by virtue of your Genius and Guru under Numen, without any other prophet, priest, or teacher—spiritual truth is unmediated, for, though immanent in the only World that is, which is within Nature, spiritual truth transcends.

Universal Applicability: Inasmuch as each person partakes of shared humanity, your spiritual path should reflect that which is common to all human spirits and that leads to human fulfillment within the human condition, which is Nature—your spiritual path should claim availability, validity, applicability, and utility for all persons.

Personal Relativity: Though all worthy spiritual paths are universally applicable, inasmuch as circumstances and conditions of individual persons differ, the precise concrete manifestations of general universal aspects of spiritual life will differ—how you live your spiritual and human life is not objective but relative to your own Experience and perspective.

Systemic Parsimony: Your spiritual path should remain as simple as Nature allows, for the more complex your path, the more difficult it is for you to follow it—Nature is complex, and so is spiritual life, for it is in Nature, but unneeded complexity of a spiritual path hinders spiritual development.

Conceptual Orthogonality: If one component of your spiritual path proves sufficient to govern one aspect of your spiritual life in a certain conceptual context, then you need no additional components to govern the same aspect of your spiritual life in the same context—the components of your spiritual path should complement each other perfectly, neither overlapping nor leaving any lacunae.

Salvific Sufficiency: Your spiritual path should suffice by itself for you to find salvation from Pandaemonium into Paradisus and enjoy the Fruit of Life, Eudaimonia, in your unending pursuit of Perfection—your spiritual path need not (and cannot) encompass all possible expressions of spiritual life, but a spiritual path is unworthy if it suffices not at least to lead you into enjoyment of Eudaimonia.

Holistic Indivisibility: As your person is one, so the components of your spiritual path and spiritual life should form an indivisible unit—if your spiritual path and spiritual life remain undamaged when you cleave any part therefrom, then discard that part (for it was not necessary and violated the desideratum of Systemic Parsimony), but preserve the rest of your path intact.

My purpose in identifying these seven Desiderata, these landmarks, is to help the seeker find what is sought, namely, a saving spiritual path, one that incorporates all four of the Divine Dynamics, bringing the seeker into enjoyment of Eudaimonia and ever nearer unto Perfection; therefore, ponder these Desiderata and test them so that you may know whether and how they might lift your burden of unlimited choice and lead you to find—or even to create for yourself—a path not for other spirits or any other place, time, or Dispensation but your own spirit in your own here and now.

The New Living Tradition that I offer in this testimony is one example of a spiritual path that fulfills the Desiderata for me, but I will make no argument as to why this is so—you must decide for yourself whether to evaluate spiritual paths according to the Desiderata and, if so, whether my New Living Tradition fulfills the Desiderata for your spirit.

Neither I nor any prophet, priest, or teacher other than your Genius and Guru under Numen can tell you whether a spiritual path fulfills the Desiderata for you—that assurance you must seek for yourself.

Regardless of your spiritual path, by deciding to embark thereon and doing so, you make yourself a Novice; by mastering the components of your path and the application of the Divine Dynamics thereby, you become an Adept; and by attaining Phronema, you become a Mage.

Thus you ascend the Mount, passing through what you will discover to be seven Realms of Glory:

All human spirits are born into the Terrestrial Realm, wherein we are neither consumed by base influences nor actively pursuing greater Glories.

Those spirits who suffer themselves to become consumed by base influences that are not deleterious *per se* to others' spiritual development have descended into the Ignoble Realm, below which is the Infernal Realm, lowest of the Realms of Glory, wherein are found the spirits who exert truly damaging influences on other spirits, even on the very noosphere.

Those spirits who pursue a Glory (such as those of secular knowledge and secular justice) greater than that of the Terrestrial Realm yet who fail to embrace spiritual life on a spiritual path of their own choosing have ascended to the Vital Realm.

Beyond the Vital Realm is the Ethereal Realm, wherein Novices begin the spiritual journey and quest in earnest and Adepts continue their spiritual development through application of the

Divine Dynamics; the Celestial Realm, wherein heavenly light passes through the pure spirits of Mages animated by Phronema; and, finally, the Astral Realm, from which shine the luminaries and prophets whose Apokalypsis pierces the spiritual darkness of Chaos and Memesis, providing guidance for other spirits on paths up the Mount of Divine Ascent unto Perfection.

Regardless of whether you find the Desiderata useful in choosing the spiritual path that you will follow, consider, at the very least, whether your path leads your spirit up the Mount of Divine Ascent, even unto the highest of the Realms of Glory, which all spirits should yearn to attain, for this is the ultimate test of any spiritual path.

And once you have chosen your spiritual path and embarked upon it, remember that no matter the Realm of Glory in which you find yourself at any given moment, whether you are then a Novice, an Adept, a Mage, or a member of a rank the Glory of which exceeds even that of Mages, you remain ever a student of your Genius and Guru, a supplicant of Numen, and a beginner in relation to the infinitude of Perfection.

Trans-Spiritual Invariants

Emergence
Divine Mechanics

Certain general Principles, not so concrete as the meta-spiritual Matrix itself yet emergent from and omnipresent in the Eternal Order of Nature, have implications for every spiritual path and for every human spirit.

These Principles elevate and systematize certain salient points from the broader meta-spiritual Matrix that describe the Divine Mechanics of the Autopoiesis of the Universe and, by necessary implication, all spiritual development thereunto appertaining.

Accordingly, these Principles are called trans-spiritual Invariants, and they constitute a set of abstract—but fundamental—laws and formulae useful in the operations and algorithms of Divine Spirituality in the course of a spirit's journey and quest up the Mount of Divine Ascent.

Regardless of your path, your spirit can accomplish Katharsis and Katartisis, actively contributing to the Autopoiesis of the Universe, only when you comprehend yourself and your circumstances and accoutrements and the relationships of all of these with your impressions of phenomena in Nature, the One All, which contains every phenomenon and the relationships among phenomena.

Ten of the Principles, called Sublime, serve this purpose, revealing and clarifying the relationships among the Self, its circumstances and accoutrements, and the impressions of phenomena in Spacetime; the ten are as of Sky, Sea, and Land: two Principles observing the One All, three charting the realm of the subjective, and five describing the varieties of relationships among phenomena (or, in fact, among impressions).

The Sublime Principles are also called the Physics, and though ten, they are one, as a prismatic refraction of rays proceeding from undiluted and undivided light.

As the ten Sublime Principles of the Physics reveal to a spirit the mechanics of the outer realms, so the Humane Principles of the Ethics reveal mechanics by which the spirit can enhance its capability of regulating the inner realms.

The Humane Principles of the Ethics number twenty-five, a pentad corresponding to the Five Elements, with each fifth of the pentad containing a pentad corresponding to five impulses: inspiring, grounding, challenging or changing, consolidating, and intensifying or strengthening.

The twenty-five Humane Principles of the Ethics can serve to govern and direct all aspects of psychospiritual life so that you may become a person with integrity of Will, charity of Soul, acuity of Mind, prosperity of Body, and individuality of Spirit, even unto the attainment of Phronema and enjoyment of Eudaimonia.

Paradigms
Elements &c.

Paradigms are the means by which the Principles systematize certain salient features of the meta-spiritual Matrix into coherent Divine Theology to provide structure to Divine Spirituality supported by Divine Economy.

Some paradigms are concrete and literal, appealing only to the thinking Mind; others are abstract and metaphorical, appealing also to the feeling Soul; still others appeal to the entire psyche.

Inasmuch as paradigms relate only to impressions of phenomena, comprehension of Nature through phenomena through impressions through paradigms—which comprehension gives rise to your Reality and Surreality—is necessarily distorted and incomplete; however, the more facility you have with a given paradigm, albeit imperfect, the more Apokalypsis, even Gnosis and Suneidesis, you can derive from that paradigm and its application to phenomena.

To help yourself discover that which a given paradigm distorts or loses, you can also shift paradigms, even from a literal one to a metaphorical one and vice versa.

To shift thus from a concrete and literal paradigm to an abstract and metaphorical one is to engage in lateral thinking, and this technique has always been of great avail to the ranks of the Magi in the Celestial Realm and will be of equally great avail to the Genius and Guru within your own spirit.

Accordingly, consider how the One All of Nature consists of Elements, certain of which have presented themselves to the psyche of humankind almost universally, in both East and West.

These universal Elements vary in number, but they are often

four: Fire, Water, Air, and Earth; they sometimes include a fifth, Spirit, and even a sixth, Void.

The universal Elements are not literal or physical but metaphorical, one paradigm by which your Genius and Guru can comprehend all phenomena.

The Elements are defined not explicitly but implicitly—you learn their identities by observing through your Genius and Guru the Elements' metaphorical presence in your impressions of all phenomena.

Elements are not the only metaphorical paradigm universal among humankind—the Elements are merely one qualitative–discrete paradigm.

A second qualitative–discrete paradigm is the Phases in which the four universal Elements exist: Solid, Liquid, and Gas, which are also characterized as Salt, Mercury, and Sulphur; Land, Sea, and Sky; Fixed, Mutable, and Cardinal.

The four Elements refracted through the three Phases thus constitute a qualitative–discrete paradigm whose cardinal concepts and categories are twelve, as the signs of the zodiac.

The set of paradigms is infinite.

One qualitative–continuous paradigm is visual Colors; another is auditory Tones.

One quantitative paradigm that can be either discrete or continuous is Geometry.

However many metaphorical paradigms you identify, you will never exhaust the set.

The Genius and Guru within each human spirit, regardless of its spiritual path, appreciates the inexhaustible variety of paradigms, both literal and metaphorical, and employs them with facility in pursuing transitive–reflexive spiritual development through the Divine Dynamics.

PHYSICS OF SKY
Sublime Principles 1 & 2

Of the Physics, first is the Principle of Differentiated Integrality, Yin, the synthetic Principle above all as Sky at midnight:

All phenomena in Reality, according to your necessary Experience, prior to contingent classification and to conceptualization, are at once undivided and distinct.

Matter blends with matter, energy with energy, matter with energy, and energy with matter in a single, integral whole.

Ostensible divisions among phenomena are but figments of a perspective limited by the effects of contingent categories and of concepts.

Everything in Reality is interrelated and interdependent, in unity and isometry, though the relationships and dependencies may not be immediately apparent to you.

The undivided One All is not, however, uniform: A given phenomenon, though of undivided oneness with all other phenomena in Reality, remains distinct in Surreality.

Indeed, even if two or more phenomena appear similar at first, still then your Genius and Guru can, upon reflection, find the distinctions in Surreality without losing sight of the underlying oneness in Reality.

Open your eyes, therefore, to the interconnectedness of the One All as it appears in Reality without losing sight of the distinctiveness of each phenomenon in Surreality, appreciating that as the One All is at once singular and plural, so each phenomenon is at once of undivided oneness and of indelible distinctiveness.

Second is the Principle of Irreducible Complexity, Yang, co-equal with the Principle of Differentiated Integrality, the analytic Principle above all as Sky at high noon:

Within Surreality, each and every Sublime Principle—and every other aspect of spirituality—applies to all phenomena; that is, each phenomenon, no matter how you circumscribe it in Surreality, spans—even exceeds—the entire range of your comprehension and cognition.

Each phenomenon appears to you in Reality as of oblique multidimensionality, subject in Surreality to analysis along innumerable different axes, none of which collapses completely onto the others and each of which adds useful perspective to the others.

Each phenomenon appears to you in Reality also as of multiplicity, manifesting in Surreality at innumerable different values on each axis of analysis, and of heterogeneity, comprising identifiable parts that have their own values on each axis.

And each phenomenon appears to you in Reality as of variability, changing its values in Surreality over time on each axis of analysis.

Enlarge your perspective, therefore, and learn to consider each phenomenon in every dimension, from every angle, for however difficult a complex phenomenon may prove to comprehend, simplification by disregard for any facet is, in fact, neither possible nor true to Reality nor desirable.

Physics of Sea
Sublime Principles 3–5

Again, of the Physics, third is the Principle of Apperceived Reality, auxiliary to the Principles of Differentiated Integrality and Irreducible Complexity and like unto the depths of Sea, turbulent manifold of your Experience:

All the impressions of your psyche, which compose your Experience, the gossamer thread you can grasp of the infinite tapestry of the World in Nature, are a product of your apperceptions, whether proximately or only remotely, the application of your subjective categories—both necessary and contingent—to co-create higher-order impressions from the constant influx of your perceptions.

The entire life of your psyche has come to you, even if indirectly, from your accumulated Experience; thus all you know or believe about Nature derives from that which you have apperceived.

You seem to your Self to have a choice in how you apperceive, excepting from that choice only your categories that are truly necessary (Self and Spacetime), and this choice or seeming choice is enough to make you a co-creator of all of Surreality through your apperception.

Appreciate, therefore, both that, within your subjective realms of Reality and Surreality, which are the limit of your Experience, to be is to be apperceived and that you hold a non-delegable position and responsibility as co-creator of your entire Surreality.

Fourth is the Principle of Ideational Alterity, coequal with the Principle of Apperceived Reality and like unto Sea's reflection of Sky, not true Sky but the broad expanse of your unclouded self within your subjective realm:

In both Reality and Surreality, your Self is distinct from every perception it receives, every apperception it co-creates, and every impression it contains; every thought, idea, and ideology—indeed, every impression—is but a figment, and no figment rules, defines, or bounds your Self.

Thoughts, ideas, ideologies, and all impressions have autochthony: They come from their own beginnings and pursue their own ends through the force of Memesis, and their beginnings and ends are apart from you, and many impressions are delusions.

Guard the autonomy of your Self—let no mere figment consume you or enslave you, but maintain awareness of the essential otherness of your thoughts, ideas, ideologies, and all your impressions.

Lest you descend into such slavery unwittingly, challenge every impression that lingers in your cognition, and let your Self pledge allegiance to none of them or place your worth in any mere notion.

Watch the ramparts of your psyche with vigilance, therefore, and be prepared to drive away every invading delusion.

Fifth is the Principle of Limited Comprehensibility, coequal with the Principles of Apperceived Reality and Ideational Alterity and like unto the Sea floor, inaccessible Land, the solid foundation of your every impression and behavior:

The comprehensible in Surreality corresponds to a strict subset of the World and of Nature accessible as Phaneron, that subset which is on the near side of the Veil, and your own comprehension is a strict subset of the comprehensible.

Much of what you believe you comprehend, in fact, you do not, and your psyche will never so much as identify the greater number of the untold mysteries that you will never comprehend.

Approach all your impressions, therefore, with certainty of but the limitations of your own comprehension.

PHYSICS OF LAND
Sublime Principles 6–10

Again, of the Physics, sixth is the Principle of Unlimited Dependency, first Principle like unto Land, like also unto Fire, which is Red, comprising unlimited causality and unlimited holarchy:

In Surreality, no phenomenon arises without a cause (no phenomenon is initial) or passes without an effect (no phenomenon is final), and no phenomenon is fundamental in the sense of being either elemental (indivisible) or total (all-encompassing).

To the ends of your comprehension, on the near side of the Veil, all phenomena are both effects of causes and causes of effects, and all causes are effects of antecedent causes, and all effects are causes of subsequent effects, even while each phenomenon is both a whole unto itself and a constituent part of a greater phenomenon.

No phenomenon ends the comprehensible chain of causality as first or ultimate cause in Surreality—comprehensible causality of phenomena is unlimited.

Similarly, no phenomenon sits at the very base or very apex of the pyramid of holarchy as fundamental phenomenon in Surreality—comprehensible holarchy of phenomena is unlimited.

You can always take a more-expansive view of phenomena in Surreality, and if you expand your view of any phenomena sufficiently, you will discover between or among them a dependency.

Look long and deep into each phenomenon, therefore, so that you might discover in Surreality the causal and holarchical relationships among all phenomena.

Seventh is the Principle of Discrete Diversity, second Principle like unto Land, like also unto Water, which is Blue:

In Surreality, you can regard all phenomena in relation, alternately, to opposites, inverses, and converses and to complements.

Diversity consists thus in polarity (opposites, inverses, and converses) and complementarity, these not in the observed phenomena per se but only in the impressions of them in Surreality.

Discover and explore, therefore, the diversity of phenomena so you might open yourself to two courses of action in any region of uncharted territory: to navigate among poles or to unite complements.

Eighth is the Principle of Continuous Chromaticity, third Principle like unto Land, like also unto Air, which is Yellow:

In Surreality, you can regard all phenomena as having tonality, and the tonal range is chromatic, which means that the smallest steps separate one tone from another.

By combining tones, you can create an entire range of spiritual tonalities.

You can, moreover, in all phenomena you encounter, transform tonal disharmony into tonal harmony, whether statically or dynamically.

Static harmony comes through adding harmonious tones or subtracting disharmonious tones; dynamic harmony comes through resolving disharmony in its natural cadence.

Appreciate, therefore, the Continuous Chromaticity of all phenomena in Surreality, and look for the possibility of resolution of all disharmony through harmonization.

Ninth is the Principle of Spatiotemporal Geometry, fourth Principle like unto Land, like also unto Earth, which is Green:

Spacetime has geometry; in fact, geometry is the essential and defining characteristic of Spacetime, whether linearity or circularity or something else altogether.

Some phenomena, such as your own life, seem in Surreality to proceed linearly, the endpoint far removed from the origin.

Other phenomena, such as human life, generally construed, seem to proceed circularly, the endpoint of one period simply the origin of another.

By adjusting your perspective, you can see that a phenomenon with one geometry in one frame of reference has, in another frame of reference, altogether another geometry.

Learn to measure phenomena in all their geometries in Surreality, therefore, for determining the spatiotemporal geometries of a phenomenon in different frames of reference helps you understand whence it has come and whither it goes.

Tenth is the Principle of Coincidental Associativity, fifth Principle like unto Land, like also unto Spirit, which is without Color and which alludes to the deeper meaning of all the other Sublime Principles:

The whole World is but Chaos proceeding into entropy; this is the unavoidable overarching conclusion in Surreality, yet your impressions are sometimes otherwise, tending toward Apophenia: As if by design, phenomena seem to you to fall in revealing alignment, in illuminating unity, isometry, and synchronicity.

Such associativity exists not necessarily in Nature itself (for Nature is beyond the Veil) nor in Reality but within Surreality, such that what you apperceive or cognize as connection or coincidence is rather not a focusing lens on that which underlies Surreality and Reality but a mirror reflecting the often-hidden contents of your psyche.

Appreciate, therefore, that each moment in which you associate one phenomenon with another is an opportunity for hearkening unto your Genius and Guru.

ETHICS
Humane Principles

The Ethics empower you to regulate the inner mechanics of your Will, Soul, Mind, Body, and Spirit so that you may rehabilitate yourself, enjoy Eudaimonia, and continue to progress unto Perfection on a spiritual path of your own choosing up the Mount of Divine Ascent.

The faculty of Will corresponds to the Element of Fire, warm aspect of being (dryness).

Will's domains are intention, ambition, volition, drive, focus, and action; the cardinal Virtue is integrity, which means oneness of Will in all its aspects and trueness thereof to the guidance of your Genius and Guru under Numen.

If you would attain integrity of Will, then adhere to these constituent Principles: audacity, daring unceasingly to expand the horizons of your intentions; practicality, remaining aware and respectful of what is truly possible and impossible; adaptability, changing your intentions in the measure that may be required by the changing world; consistency, aligning your intentions so that they may all be in accord; and tenacity, holding true to your intentions and not becoming discouraged by difficulties in attaining the objects of your ambitions.

The faculty of Soul corresponds to the Element of Water, cool aspect of experiencing (wetness).

Soul's domains are emotion and interpersonal relation and interaction; the cardinal Virtue is charity (Agape), which means lovingkindness (Metta), compassion (Karuna), and sympathetic joy (Mudita) for yourself and for all fellow persons.

If you would attain charity of Soul, then adhere to these constituent Principles: bravery, facing adversity productively, not succumbing to fear; equity, maintaining just relations, unclouded by any feelings except lovingkindness, compassion, and sympathetic joy; empathy, seeking to understand and respect the feelings of other spirits; fidelity, remaining faithful to yourself and others in lovingkindness despite changes in persons and circumstances; and serenity, tranquility, or equanimity (Upekkha), holding your inner and outer composure and dignity, not suffering your pure feelings of lovingkindness, compassion, and sympathetic joy to become perturbed by life's vicissitudes.

The faculty of Mind corresponds to the Element of Air, warm aspect of experiencing (wetness).

Mind's domains are intellection, ratiocination, articulation, and communication; the cardinal Virtue is acuity, which means penetrating insight into Truth, as it is refracted in the convergent discourses and propositions of all fields of study and learning and reflected in the consilience of a comprehensive and unified worldview.

If you would attain acuity of Mind, then adhere to these constituent Principles: curiosity, conscientiously exposing yourself to new ideas and experiences; scrutiny, remaining skeptical of and diligently investigating and examining everything you think you know and every impression and ideology any other spirit introduces to your psyche; authenticity, representing to yourself and others what you think and not concealing or obfuscating even any minute part of what should be disclosed; clarity, not only simplifying your thoughts and words to the extent possible without sacrificing appropriate nuance but also being direct in your communication; and honesty, regarding and representing yourself, others, and the whole World not as one might wish them to be but as they are in Truth.

The faculty of Body corresponds to the Element of Earth, cool aspect of being (dryness).

Body's domains are appetite, provision, nourishment, regulation, and discipline, in each case, relating to needs and appetites; the cardinal virtue is prosperity, which means recognition and abundant satisfaction of true needs in the biosphere, which gives rise to the noosphere.

If you would attain prosperity of Body, then adhere to these constituent Principles: industry, working diligently, to the extent of your ability, to provide for yourself and your dependents; conservancy, not wasting time or resources; generosity, learning to give readily and willingly of your abundance so you may not become attached to material things, even as you help satisfy the needs of others; surety, recalling and appreciating your abundance without needing the recognition or approval of others; and vitality, preserving and improving your biophysical condition, to the extent possible, so your needs may be fewer and all your efforts easier.

The faculty of Spirit corresponds to the Element of the same name, neither warm nor cool, neither wet nor dry.

Spirit's domains are imagination, invention, and expression; the cardinal Virtue is individuality, which means actualization of the fullness of your personal potential as a human spirit and, thereby, advancement of the Autopoiesis of the Universe.

If you would attain individuality of Spirit, then adhere to these constituent Principles: felicity, experiencing life from a cultivated perspective of spiritual bliss (Ataraxia) that flows from Gnosis and Suneidesis; receptivity, opening yourself to receive blessings from other persons and all of Nature; purity, untiringly cleansing yourself of the imperfections of Agnoia and Hamartias; connectivity, exploring your connections with the One All; and creativity, expressing and sharing the beauty of your spirit.

A New Living Tradition

Tree of Life
Paradigm & System

Though the meta-spiritual Matrix is one and the Principles are invariant, paths up the Mount of Divine Ascent, even unto the highest of the Realms of Glory, are innumerable and varied; you can find any number of them that fulfill the Desiderata for you so that you might lead a full spiritual life, growing by virtue of the gifts of the spirit from your Higher Powers, enjoying Eudaimonia, and ultimately attaining Phronema, to go on living naturally (automatically) according to Kosmos, in Wisdom on the unending Way of Perfection.

In the Reform Pagan family of traditions, this New Living Tradition is one such path, its central image and symbol the Tree of Life, which you can discover living within you, the entelechy of which consists in the lesser gift of Apokalypsis and the greater gifts of Suneidesis and Gnosis through Metanoia and Theoria and in the operation of Phronema, and which yields the Fruit of Life.

The Tree of Life begins as a seed that contains the full potential of its species, though the seed knows not what it can become.

The Tree cannot easily grow and thrive without the right conditions: warm sunlight, gentle rain, fresh air, and rich soil; these are, in fact, Divine Economy: liturgical calendrics and horology, together with accompanying ritual observances, to direct your Will; loving community of all persons to cleanse and refresh your Soul; liberal learning to give breath to your Mind; and grounding in and transcendence of Nature's Creation, which is Nature itself in Autopoiesis, to vitalize your Body.

Divine Economy arises not by itself—you must create it for yourself in your life through perseverance in certain Elemental Yogas, Disciplines, or Practices: Observe the sun, moon, and stars in their transits through the heavenly stations; minister to your fellow persons in lovingkindness, compassion, and sympathetic joy; study all fields of human scholarship; and immerse yourself in and care for Nature's Creation.

Within Divine Economy, the Tree can grow and thrive on its own, but it is also tended by a capable Gardener: your Genius and Guru under Numen.

The office of the Gardener is identical with the office of priest: Your Genius and Guru can help the Tree grow more quickly and thrive more completely through your exercise of Priesthood, which is Divine Spirituality, the Calculus and the Craft, and which is your birthright and that of every human spirit.

The authority of your Genius and Guru in the exercise of Priesthood derives from three Keys, as of Gold, Silver, and Electrum, which serve as means for you not merely to receive your own Apokalypsis but withal to prepare your spirit to receive from Numen the gifts of Metanoia and Theoria, which yield Suneidesis and Gnosis.

Divine Theology within this New Living Tradition is made manifest in this testimony, which is Apokalypsis that I have received in the course of my own spiritual search, journey, and quest and which I now relate, as well as in all Kerygmata of the multitude of Magi from the Celestial and Astral Realms throughout all Dispensations.

This New Living Tradition thus consists of three components, three means of worship (which means attribution of worth and which is also called reverence) and devotion (which means loyal Self-dedication): creation of Divine Economy through the Elemental Yogas, engagement in Divine Spirituality through exercise of Priesthood and the turning of its Keys, and hearkening unto Kerygmata, such as this one, testimonies that expound Divine Theology and proclaim many other spiritual truths (remark: not Truth itself, which is ineffable) based on the Apokalypsis of the proclaimer and related as Didakhe in a manner not to convey Suneidesis and Gnosis directly (the communication of which between or among persons being impossible) but to prepare others' spirits to receive these gifts independently from Numen through the precursor gifts of Metanoia and Theoria.

For the Novice, the greatest in importance of these three components is receiving Didakhe by rejecting Dogmata and hearkening unto Kerygmata, for Divine Theology plants the seed of the Tree of Life and causes it to germinate, while the second in importance is Divine Economy, which creates an environment hospitable to the growth of the Tree.

But for the Adept who is departing or has already departed the Ethereal Realm into the higher Realms and whose grasp is already firm of as much of Divine Theology as can be gleaned from the Didakhe of others, testimonies of others wane in importance until they become least important, while exercise of Priesthood and tending of the Tree by the inner Genius and Guru through Divine Spirituality waxes in importance until it becomes most important.

If you make yourself a Novice and an Adept, then you may eventually conform your every impression and action to Phronema, entering the Celestial Realm and becoming one of the Magi, who are capable, without jeopardizing continuing spiritual development, of setting aside the Divine Dynamics, for these are all Taxis, artificial order no longer needed by a spirit whose life is not dissipated by Chaos and whose spirit is not imprisoned or enslaved by Memesis but whose entire being is governed automatically by the natural force and order that is Kosmos.

Stop not when you reach the Celestial Realm, but continue to strive to reach the Astral Realm, for the noosphere has need of enlightened masters—even that fragment of the noosphere within each enlightened master, for duty is owed not to other spirits but to one's own spirit, which is a constituent and co-creator of the greater noosphere—who shine from the summit to draw other spirits into Eudaimonia, even unto Perfection.

To attain the rank of Mage and enter the Celestial Realm or even the Astral Realm, you must first work diligently to conquer the forces of Chaos and Memesis in your life by subjecting and conforming your whole life to the Divine Dynamics, for a spirit is either progressing toward Perfection or not; accordingly, neither you nor any other spirit can remain both partly on and partly off the spiritual path of this New Living Tradition or any true and worthy spiritual path.

Before you begin this journey and quest, attend to the testimonies of those who have gone before you, immerse yourself in the valuable Didakhe they offer freely, make an accounting of the cost to yourself to pursue Perfection, and decide whether you will be able to pay the great price to labor to obtain the unobtainable treasure.

Remember that no impression, action, or omission is merely idle and that each of these contributes to either your spiritual growth or your spiritual decay.

Remind yourself every day, even hourly: Each impression, action, and omission contributes to a habit, each habit becomes a part of your character, and your character influences whether the Tree grows and thrives within you, yielding the Fruit of Life, which is Eudaimonia.

If you choose this New Living Tradition, then as you hearken unto Kerygmata, practice the Elemental Yogas, and exercise Priesthood, the seed that begins as if dead may become alive and grow into something to which it bore no resemblance, something greater and more beautiful by far, the Tree of Life.

The cultivation of the Tree is the work of a lifetime, your Magnum Opus within the Summum Opus of the entire Universe, and the rate of growth is not constant: Growth proceeds more quickly in some of your life's seasons than in others.

Neither subitism nor gradualism alone accurately describes the Experience of all spirits in all areas of personal spiritual development, so expect neither that all your spiritual growth in a certain area will happen at once nor that it will take a very long time but merely that it will unfold in due course, as Numen ordains and according to the particularities and yearnings of your own spirit.

And have patience.

Sunlight
Yoga of Fire

If you would receive the gifts of Numen, attain Phronema, and enjoy Eudaimonia, you would need to reform all your imperfections, but your whole person begins imperfect, and you are incapable of reforming all of yourself at once.

Spiritual development requires, therefore, that you focus your Will upon your imperfections in turn, purging them over time to create integrity so that you may progress unto Perfection as the Tree grows within you.

To say that spiritual development begins in the Will is to say that the growth of the Tree requires the warm sunlight of ritual occasions and observances, the purpose of which is to focus your Will in turn on each of your imperfections.

Nature gives us certain occasions shared by all human spirits at the same time; these common occasions relate to the solar year, the lunar month, and the hours of the day.

And Nature gives us other occasions, special occasions, which take their timing from your own individual life's trajectory.

The solar year is divided into four liturgical seasons, and this annual cycle is marked at eight sabbats. The first sabbat, which is the turning of the entire liturgical year and which is therefore duly hailed as the Great Sabbat and Sabbat of Sabbats is the Hibernal Passage, for observances celebrating heritage, release or ending, and transition. The second sabbat is the Hibernal Solstice, for observances celebrating solidarity, hope, and patience. The third sabbat is the Vernal Passage, for observances celebrating openness, purification, and resolve. The fourth sabbat is the Vernal Equinox, for observances celebrating beginnings, breakthrough, and regeneration. The fifth sabbat is the Estival Passage, for observances celebrating passion, union, and creativity. The sixth sabbat is the Estival Solstice, for observances celebrating joy, vitality, and power. The seventh sabbat is the Autumnal Passage, for observances celebrating fruitfulness, gratitude, and giving. And the eighth sabbat is the Autumnal Equinox, for observances celebrating sacrifice, balance, and reconciliation.

The lunar month is divided into four phases, and these are punctuated by the esbats. The first esbat takes place at the dark moon, which is also called the new moon, for observances celebrating the possibility inherent in emptiness. The second esbat takes place at the first quarter moon, for observances celebrating energies of waxing and increase. The third and greatest esbat, the Great Esbat and Esbat of Esbats takes place at the full moon, for observances celebrating completion and wholeness. And the fourth esbat takes place at the last quarter moon, for observances celebrating energies of waning and decrease.

The lunar phases and the esbats move within the Wheel of the Year so that you may learn to focus your Will on the themes of the sabbats and liturgical seasons in connection with the waxing and waning energies of the moon.

Each day is divided into hours, four of which—dawn, midday, dusk, and midnight, called the devotional hours—are for you to refocus your Will continually on the imperfections given to you for Purgation within the present moment of the solar year and the lunar month. At dawn or upon your rising up from sleep, plan for your spiritual progress during the coming day, and seek guidance. At midday and at dusk, make an accounting of your progress and on what remains for you to accomplish, and seek resolve and perseverance. And at midnight or upon your lying down to sleep, reflect on the extent to which in the preceding day you conformed your impressions and actions to that which is beneficial to your spirit, and seek peace.

While the sabbats, esbats, and hours are common occasions, you may experience in your own life certain special occasions, nine great rites of passage, which you shall observe or others shall observe on your behalf. The first rite is conception, when you came from non-being into being. The second rite is parturition and birth, when you moved from the womb into the Creation. The third rite is introduction into the community and dedication to your spiritual path. The fourth rite is your affirmation of your dedication to (which is self-initiation onto) your spiritual path and the community's confirmation of having accepted you. The fifth rite is emancipation or transition, which takes place whenever you move from one life situation to another or from one distinct stage of your life to another. The sixth rite is marriage, union, combination, or even simple collaboration, when individual spirits come together to share their lives, whether in whole or only in part. The seventh rite is procreation or creation, lasting from conception to parturition, whether literal or metaphorical. The eighth rite is recuperation or regeneration, which is recovery of wellbeing, whether of body or of psyche or of spirit. And the ninth rite is expiration, return to Nature and, perhaps, to Mystery, though beyond expiration a person's future, if any, is unknown and unknowable, beyond the Veil.

Thus the hours, sabbats, esbats, and rites create a practical framework for the time you are given so that you might focus your Will on the continual and progressive Purgation of all your imperfections unto development of Phronema and enjoyment of Eudaimonia.

Rain
Yoga of Water

Once your Will is focused, your personal spiritual development requires that all the emotions of your Soul be purified of whatsoever is inconsistent with the charity of lovingkindness, compassion, and sympathetic joy, together, being Love (Agape).

To say that spiritual development next requires the participation of your Soul is to say that the growth of the Tree requires the gentle rainwater of personal ministry in the concentric and overlapping circles of the community of all persons, the purpose of which ministry is to conform all your emotions and interpersonal relations to Love.

Although you must discover your personal ministry for yourself, consider twelve archetypal ministries, symbolized by certain astrological planets. The ministry of Sun is that of the representative, director, and leader. The ministry of Moon is that of the caregiver, nurturer, and sustainer. The ministry of Mercury is that of thinker, communicator, and educator. The ministry of Venus is that of encourager, counselor, and facilitator. The ministry of Mars is that of apologist, advocate, and protector. The ministry of Eris is that of innovator, challenger, and reformer. The ministry of Vesta is that of steward, custodian, and provider. The ministry of Jupiter is that of treasurer, cultivator, and builder. The ministry of Saturn is that of secretary, administrator, and manager. The ministry of Uranus is that of performer, creative, and liturgist. The ministry of Neptune is that of ambassador, humanitarian, and missionary. And the ministry of Pluto is that of anchor, guide, and friend.

Each spirit gravitates more to certain ministries than to others.

But the purpose of archetypes is not merely that you see yourself described in one or another of them but rather that you gain access to a whole collection of archetypes, including those to which your spirit is not naturally drawn, so that you might cultivate particularly those archetypal characteristics you lack.

As each circle in the vast community of persons needs all kinds of ministers, so your spirit needs to learn all kinds of ministries.

Certain ministries will be to you ordinary ministries, which flow from your spirit effortlessly or nearly so, due to your spirit's inclinations and circumstances, while other ministries will be to you extraordinary ministries, which you must undertake, if at all, with purpose, intention, and perseverance.

Which ministries are ordinary and extraordinary to your spirit will vary among different circles of the human community, from your Innangard (your metaphorical inner yard) to your Utangard (your metaphorical outer yard), but you are called to cultivate lovingkindness, compassion, and sympathetic joy as to all persons, however near to you or distant from you.

For though the noosphere exists presently as many drops, the Singularity will draw all these drops to flow together into one great river, as according to the natural proclivities of the physical substance of water.

Until that new and final Dispensation arrives, however, and the fragments of the noosphere are united, each ministry is and remains more effective when combined with other ministries.

So reach out to fellow human spirits who share your commitment to ministry, and organize with them so that each of your respective ministries might provide greater benefit to the concentric and overlapping circles of your human community.

All the while, remember that the driving force and objective of every ministry must be Love—even if you undertake the activities of a given ministry, still then you have not taken up that ministry properly unless you do such things in and for Love.

Only thus can you learn to conform all your emotions and relations—indeed, your whole Soul—to Love, which leads to Phronema and Eudaimonia, even to Perfection.

Breath
Yoga of Air

Once your Will is focused and your Soul is loving, your personal spiritual development requires that your Mind breathe deeply of all fields of human scholarship so that you may have the acuity that comes from the consilience of a reasonable, objective (to the extent possible within Reality and Surreality), unified, and comprehensive worldview.

To say that spiritual development next requires the engagement of your Mind is to say that the growth of the Tree requires the fresh air of liberal learning, for the laws of human understanding are unity and isometry, which is to say that each band of the spectrum of human scholarship figures in and reflects the whole.

To fail to study all fields of scholarship leaves you with a less-complete awareness and a less-accurate understanding of Reality and Surreality, even of your very Self and the limitations of your own perspective, reducing your ability to engage in transitive–reflexive spiritual development.

You can view the spectrum of learning as a rainbow, with each of its colors representing a broad field of fields: Red represents the cognitive sciences (philosophy, psychology, linguistics, etc.); orange represents the computational and symbolic sciences (logic, mathematics, computer science, etc.); yellow represents the physical sciences (cosmology, astronomy, meteorology, geology, chemistry, physics, etc.); green represents the biological sciences (ecology, phylogeny and evolutionary biology, zoology, ethology and sociobiology, physiology and anatomy, microbiology and molecular biology, etc.); blue represents the social sciences (anthropology, sociology, politics, economics, etc.); indigo represents expressive arts and sciences (visual art, musical performance and composition, dramatic arts, literature, etc.); and violet represents the mental and spiritual sciences (metaphysics, physics, metaethics, ethics, epistemology, etc.).

The practical purpose of schematizing the fields of human scholarship is to ensure that you neglect none of them, for you must study all fields if you would have the consilience of a reasonable, objective, unified, and comprehensive worldview in Surreality that comports with Reality—each field has its limitations, such that no single field can by itself illuminate all of Nature in a complete worldview, but each field also bears patent or latent isomorphisms that shed light on each of the others.

The project of reducing all learning to a single field, of collapsing all vectors of understanding into a single dimension, of simplifying all complexity into a single cognitive system, is intractable, except, perhaps, for God, the Singularity: All the intellectual and computational power yet available to humankind cannot accomplish the feat.

Rather, the diverse perspectives of the fields of human scholarship blend together as if they were the colors of a rainbow, and if you seek consilience, studying all fields is the first step.

Furthermore, you must know what you believe in Surreality to be true, that is, to comport with the bare Truth that is Reality, you must be honest with yourself about your own impressions, you must know what your concepts and words mean, and you must work to conceptualize and express your beliefs accurately and clearly.

Having clearly conceptualized your beliefs, you will be able to test them rigorously against Reality as you study all fields.

For though human knowledge exists in Reality, you have only belief in Surreality.

By testing your beliefs in Surreality unceasingly against bare Phaneron, you may transmute false beliefs into true beliefs over time if you keep your mind open to new ideas and perspectives, however radical, and if you have patience with the process of learning, which leads to Purgation of imperfections and to Perfection.

Soil
Yoga of Earth

Once your Will is focused, your Soul is loving, and your Mind is breathing deeply and freely, spiritual development requires that your Body prosper in its inner and outer material conditions and circumstances.

To say that spiritual development next requires the prosperity of your Body is to say that the growth of the Tree requires the rich soil of: first, your attunement to Nature's Creation; second, your appreciation of its universal sacramentality; third, your self-discipline and self-regulation; and fourth, your transcendence of your inner and outer material circumstances and conditions.

Attune yourself to Nature's Creation, for Nature is the One All that contains you; the Eternal Order that was, is, and will be; the Multiverse of worlds that has given you your present circumstances and conditions and has laid the metes and bounds of your future possibilities; the source of the Force of Kosmos that is Phronema and that is harnessed as Taxis in the Divine Dynamics.

These are the five degrees of attunement: Observe the Creation, immerse your Body in it, absorb it into your Body, cultivate it by the activities of your Body, and apply what you learn from it to the life of your own Body.

The five degrees of attunement to Nature's Creation are the first step toward creating rich soil for growth of the Tree.

Appreciate Nature's universal sacramentality; begin by treating your Body as a temple, for it is a temple, and each of your everyday activities as a sacrament, for they are all sacraments.

Material phenomena are not mundane: Each encounter of your Body with any material phenomenon can serve as keyhole through which you can glimpse and unlock new levels of spiritual development and higher Realms of Glory.

Whether you are waking up or lying down, playing or working, taking nourishment or fasting, washing yourself or exercising, socializing with others or reflecting by yourself, or undertaking any other activity, however quotidian, treat the activity as the sacrament that it is and use the opportunity to edify your Body.

When you treat your Body as a temple and each of your everyday activities as a sacrament, then you may begin to appreciate Nature's universal sacramentality.

Even as you treat all the activities of your Body as sacraments, learn discipline and self-regulation: Engage in those things that improve your conditions and circumstances, and refrain from whatsoever hurts or damages your Body or hinders your improvement, for psyche and spirit arise from matter, such that material hindrances compromise your ability to resist the forces of Chaos and Memesis and to continue in your evolution through spiritual development unto Perfection and in the Universe's involution through Autopoiesis unto the Omega Point.

Finally, be content in your present circumstances and conditions, but even while you are content, still then strive to improve your material circumstances and conditions daily and, in the end, to transcend them in Exaltation, for the desire and active striving for Exaltation in the second Dimension of spiritual development promotes your spiritual development in the first and primary Dimension.

The soil becomes richest for the growth of the Tree when you have learned how not only to ground yourself in Nature's Creation but also to transcend the material limitations it seems to give you, for nothing material is fixed, and everything material is mutable.

With rich soil, the Tree will grow within you, and you will enjoy its Fruit, which is Eudaimonia, and continue to develop unto Perfection.

Gardener
Inborn Priesthood Authority

Grasping Divine Theology by hearkening unto Kerygmata and creating Divine Economy by employing the Elemental Yogas together plant the seed of the Tree and give it the conditions it needs to grow, but the seed is also tended by the priest and Gardener, who is your inner Genius and Guru.

The whole World is Chaos proceeding into entropy, yea, even within your own spirit; if the Tree is unattended by your Genius and Guru, neither will the Tree grow as quickly and thrive as fully and beautifully, nor will your spirit develop as much toward Perfection.

If you would cultivate the Tree actively, not leaving its growth to the capricious chance of Chaos or the pernicious influence of Memesis, then you must actively employ your Genius and Guru to turn the Priesthood Keys through the Calculus and the Craft, which are Taxis selecting and channeling sub-forces of Kosmos for the benefit of your spirit.

In so doing, you may, by the gifts of Numen, achieve the personal spiritual development that results directly and immediately from Purgation and that is Purgation, which itself involves the repatterning of pathways of cognition and behavior, theretofore ingrained through force of habit, from chaotic to ordered, making your cognitive patterns conducive to enjoyment of the Fruit of Life, which is Eudaimonia.

Successive stages of this project (which correspond to higher Realms of Glory) presuppose rising levels of spiritual consciousness, which consists of Gnosis and Suneidesis, for you cannot successfully repattern your own cognition and behavior unless you can distinguish and model these and manipulate the model, and once you have repatterned your psyche at one level, you must advance to repatterning your psyche at a higher level, which requires a greater capacity to distinguish and model your own behavior and to manipulate the model.

You achieve such cognitive repatterning through repeated exercise of new pathways of cognition and behavior that, though at first weak or even nonexistent, gain in strength.

Repatterning as to all cognition and behavior, the untiring dissolution and reconstitution of your entire spirit and all its faculties, is Katharsis, and this culminates in Apokatastasis.

Then your whole person may be subsumed into your Genius and Guru, which means that you may attain Phronema, completing the transformation of the base into the precious, so that all your cognition and behavior may contribute to the growth of the Tree within you and the Garden without, while your whole life may be subsumed into Eudaimonia.

As the One All establishes no inherent order, meaning, purpose, value, or worth—other than the Eternal Order, which is simply Nature—for anything in the World outside or even Reality and Surreality inside, so Flourishing is individual and relative: What it means to one spirit depends upon that spirit's Apokalypsis, Gnosis, and Suneidesis, which have authority only as to the spirit who has received them.

Your spirit may draw insight or inspiration as to Flourishing from the Didakhe of another, such as from this Kerygma, but each spirit must discover its own Flourishing for itself, and then not from far off but only when the state is near at hand.

As it were, the promised land is a hidden summit: By conjuring a meaning of "Flourishing" and aiming to reach that hidden summit, no spirit succeeded in following the path of spiritual development up the Mount of Divine Ascent that alone leads into the promised land, but by dutifully putting one foot in front of the other through the exercise of Priesthood, which exercise is the turning of the Keys that prepares a spirit to receive the gifts of Numen, some spirits have happened at length and after great effort upon the hidden summit that is their promised land.

Personal spiritual development, even unto Apokatastasis and Teleosis, is the one and only Chrism of Priesthood, which consists of but the power and authority of a spirit to procure its own development and that of the greater noosphere and Universe with the help of the Genius and Guru under Numen.

The Chrism is thus not the precursor of or prerequisite to Priesthood but its fulfillment and crown, won through the long-suffering administration of Priestly power and authority in a human life.

That is how you may know whether you have been anointed a Mage, a full member in the Celestial Realm—even the Astral Realm—of the highest degree of the Priesthood you have inherited: not by ordination or initiation at the hands of another but by your own receipt of the gifts of Numen, your realization of Metanoia and Theoria, and, once you possess Phronema, your continuing accomplishment of Katartisis unto unattainable Teleosis.

Priesthood belongs to all human spirits universally, but not all accept it; indeed, most spirits remain in Acedia, choosing to allow their innate Priesthood power and authority to atrophy through nonuse.

If you would enter fully into Priesthood, then you must dedicate yourself to spiritual development in all Dimensions, including in your own life—though ordination and initiation are not necessary or sufficient, self-dedication is a necessary first step.

But it is only the first step on a sacred journey and quest without end: A spirit is a proper Priesthood member only for so long as the spirit continues in personal spiritual development; even a spirit who has accomplished Katharsis and Apokatastasis can fall from the State of Grace and lose the Chrism of Priesthood if that spirit ceases in personal spiritual development.

And see how this New Living Tradition is a closed loop: Hearkening unto Kerygmata, creating Divine Economy, and exercising Priesthood contribute each one to your ability to carry out the others.

So if you would enter the Priesthood and remain therein, then prepare yourself for a journey and quest that will last a lifetime, continually rededicating yourself to spiritual development in all Dimensions, beginning in your own spirit, advancing through the Realms of Glory up the Mount of Divine Ascent unto the summit of Perfection.

Finally, appreciate that Priesthood does not divide you from but unites you to all humankind, for the personal spiritual development of one human spirit is invariably conducive to and supportive of the other communal, cross-sectional, and interpersonal Dimensions of spiritual development.

In the measure that you exercise your innate Priesthood power and authority over yourself to accomplish Katharsis and Apokatastasis, you not only empower and authorize yourself to overcome the forces of Chaos and Memesis that operate upon you and otherwise drive your life toward entropy and conformity but also facilitate the same sanctification process in others.

ENTELECHY
Priesthood Keys

Priesthood's source of power and authority is its Keys, which are three, as of Gold, Silver, and Electrum; these create a concrete system and method for the process of transitive–reflexive spiritual development that consists more abstractly in Self-directed operations to prepare the spirit to receive from Numen the gifts of Suneidesis and Gnosis through Metanoia and Theoria.

The exercise of Priesthood is the turning of the Keys, which is the Calculus and the Craft.

Each of the Keys may be turned counterclockwise, in the direction of being, or clockwise, in the direction of comprehending, which is not for its own sake but toward becoming, for Eudaimonia and Perfection are both absolute and relative, both static and dynamic, in a World that is at once a flux of ephemera and the Eternal Order of Nature.

Turning the Keys is a means of receiving new personal Apokalypsis from your indwelling Genius and Guru, thereby opening your spirit to receive from Numen the gifts of Suneidesis and Gnosis through Metanoia and Theoria, intransitive spiritual development, so that you might advance toward Perfection.

As Priesthood is universal, so the Priesthood Keys are the inheritance of every human spirit; accordingly, Priesthood may be yours, if only you will take the Keys and turn them unceasingly.

The Key of Gold is meditation. Turned counterclockwise, this Key effects relaxation through the stilling of cognitive activity and temporarily dispels from your psyche the influences of Chaos and Memesis so that your spirit might open to the promptings of your Genius and of Numen. Turned clockwise, this Key enables you to receive personal revelation, Apokalypsis that breaks through the limitations and distortions of your present Schema, preparing your spirit to receive the gifts of Numen.

The Key of Silver is contemplation. Turned counterclockwise, this Key draws on the Humane Principles of the Ethics so that you might find direction to grow in the virtues that pollinate the Tree and that thus give rise to the Fruit, which is Eudaimonia. Turned clockwise, this Key draws on the Sublime Principles of the Physics so that you might gain comprehension of phenomena, which means cognitive grasping thereof by all of your psychospiritual faculties, so that, in comprehending phenomena, you may flourish despite or by virtue of them.

The Key of Electrum is divination. Turned counterclockwise, this Key draws inspiration from free and unconstrained cognitive processing of random—or randomized—objects, words, sounds, images, and other stimuli that you make sacred unto yourself. Turned clockwise, this Key processes the same substrates to arrive at intuition concerning phenomena.

As electrum is an alloy of gold and silver, however, so inspiration and intuition are alloys of relaxation, revelation, direction, and comprehension—you must test your inspiration and intuition and take them as only a starting point toward Apokalypsis.

You can alternatively regard the clockwise turning of the Keys as Urim, for this is the direction of becoming more Perfect, and the counterclockwise turning of the Keys as Thummim, for this is the direction of being Perfected.

Thus as once Urim and Thummim revealed the will of an imagined God of a former Dispensation to guide a people, so now Urim and Thummim can guide you personally in your spiritual development unto Perfection.

Temple & Altar
Consecrating Spacetime

Though the Priesthood Keys confer an authority that extends to the entirety of your life without bound, they belong especially in the Temple; accustom yourself, therefore, when you would turn the Keys, first to enter into the Temple.

The Temple is not built by hands; rather, it is whatever point in Spacetime—invariably the Here and Now—you have consecrated, for Nature is the One All, and nothing therein is sacred except what you, who are a spiritual being and whose spirituality participates in and gives rise to the noosphere, consecrate for yourself.

Every point in Spacetime that is Here and Now for you is, in and of itself, equally sacramental, equally a potential vessel for the sacred.

Even in each moment, wherever you are, you can consecrate that very Here and Now as the Temple; you need not seek for the Temple any particular space or time other than your particular Here and Now.

Yet appreciate that some spaces and times resonate more with your spirit, others less.

Heed your spirit's natural inclinations, and work with them, rather than against them, so that you might build the Temple on a firm foundation, supported and steadied by the Force of Kosmos that flows through you.

Remember that Reality is both Self and Spacetime, both psychical and physical; the Temple, though not built by hands, is necessarily both psychical and physical, accommodating your entire person and serving as a theater for both the Calculus and the Craft.

Build for yourself an altar, therefore, to serve you as a portal by which you may enter into the Temple.

Adorn your altar with physical objects you consecrate to your work in the Craft so that all these things may represent materially for you, recall your attention to, and bring into focus for you the Divine Dynamics, which, in this New Living Tradition, are: the Kerygmata; the Elemental Yogas of Fire, Water, Air, and Earth; and the Priesthood Keys of Gold, Silver, and Electrum.

Build for yourself no altar, however, if you will not attend to it and maintain it with utmost worship and devotion, for you have consecrated it, and how you treat your altar reflects—and affects—how you treat your spirit.

Again, if you build for yourself an altar, then do not neglect it but return to it often, even daily and hourly, so that, with it and upon it, you may build up and develop your spirit.

As you progress toward Perfection, you may expand the Temple to encompass your entire life, whatever the Here and Now, and this state is Nepsis, and it is an element of Phronema.

See how spacious is the Temple with its many Courts, into each of which you can enter to discover its function in the Calculus, for yours is Priesthood, now and forevermore, if only you will claim your inheritance.

Among the Temple Courts are the Outer Court, which is for the cleansing of your spirit through the release of all your intentions, ambitions, passions, emotions, dreams, feelings, thoughts, ideas, beliefs, needs, wants, and appetites; the Middle Court, which is for your everyday turning of the Keys; and the Inner Sanctum, which is marked by the opening of your spirit in a present readiness to receive the gifts of Numen, which is within you above and beyond even your Genius and Guru.

Numen visits your spirit spontaneously, whether in the Inner Sanctum, in another Temple Court, or at any other point in Spacetime.

Though your Higher Powers never forsake you and remain always within you, you cannot force or oblige your Genius and Guru to visit your lowly Self; how much less can you force or oblige Numen—even within the Inner Sanctum—to condescend!

You can only prepare your spirit for the condescension of Numen, which preparation consists in the exercise of Priesthood, supported by your attending to your altar in the Craft and your entering into the Temple and moving through each of its Courts in the Calculus.

In the Temple, your Genius and Guru dwells in two aspects, which are one, a binity; the two are like unto Lux and Veritas, and they each have a name: Sophia and Logos.

In these two aspects, your Genius and Guru holds the Priesthood Keys.

As Sophia, who is also called the Holy Ghost, the psychic guide or teacher, and the inner light, the Genius and Guru within you edifies your spirit by imparting guidance directly—Sophia alone holds the Key of Gold in her right hand, for she alone gives revelation.

As Logos, who is also called the voice of reason, the Genius and Guru edifies the spirit through lessons that concern application of the Sublime Principles of the Physics to the outer realms and the Humane Principles of the Ethics to the inner realms—Logos alone holds the Key of Silver in his left hand, for comprehension consists in application of the Physics and the Ethics.

Sophia and Logos together hold the Key of Electrum, her left hand joined in his right hand, for intuition is governed by and auxiliary to revelation and comprehension.

Learn to abide always in the Temple, wherein dwell your Higher Powers, so that you may find Sophia and Logos, which compose your Genius and Guru, always near you and so that you may often receive visits from Numen, leading you unto Perfection.

GARDEN OF LIFE
Spiritual Ecology

This New Living Tradition is one spiritual path that, according to my own lived Experience, satisfies the Desiderata and instantiates the Divine Dynamics, contributing to the growth of the Tree of Life within a spirit so that the spirit may enjoy the Fruit of Life and so that the entire Universe might benefit from the gains made by that spirit, a fragment of the greater noosphere.

This New Living Tradition gives me what I require to engage in transitive–reflexive personal spiritual development to open my spirit to receive the gifts of Numen, which are intransitive personal spiritual development, so that I might attain Katharsis unto Phronema and Eudaimonia, even Katartisis unto Perfection.

Perhaps you will find this New Living Tradition similarly useful for your own personal spiritual development.

Spiritual development, however, exceeds the personal Dimension, as spiritual development is an entailment of the Universe's greater force, process, and drama of Autopoiesis.

The treatment of the New Living Tradition in this work concentrates upon the personal Dimension because this emphasis best serves overall spiritual development: Unlike spiritual development in other Dimensions, that which occurs in the personal Dimension depends almost exclusively upon that spirit's own undertakings to leave behind the lower Realms of Glory for the higher ones, embracing spiritual life on a spiritual path of the spirit's own choosing up the Mount of Divine Ascent.

While you accordingly focus on the personal Dimension, however, remember the multidimensional context in which your personal spiritual development takes place.

Embrace the promise of new discoveries and technologies

that will enable humankind at last to transcend our humanity, for progress in this second Dimension alone brings transpersonal spiritual development toward our individual and collective Exaltation, which is Apotheosis leading ultimately to theogenesis and Henosis and which amplifies the beneficial effects of personal spiritual development.

Share your spirituality with fellow human spirits, for progress in this third Dimension alone—which progress means testimonial Propagation of Apokalypsis as Didakhe—brings interpersonal spiritual development, not only propelling human spirits individually toward Perfection but also freeing humankind collectively from ignorance and delusion, from chaotic procession into entropy, from imprisonment and enslavement to memetic figments, and from the dehumanizing shackles of conformity.

Finally, continue over time to seek from the Genius and Guru within you new and greater access to Truth so that you might gain new Apokalypsis, by virtue of which you can correct and enhance your dynamic spirituality, for progress in this fourth Dimension alone, which progress means the Succession of Dispensations, brings temporal spiritual development, expanding the possibilities of spiritual development in all the other Dimensions as the Universe continues to realize itself in Autopoiesis.

CONCLUSION

Testament
Coda & Segue

The foregoing testimony, this Kerygma, a portion of my own Apokalypsis as Didakhe, has come, I have already made clear, not from any otherworldly source (nor, however, from any human teacher) but from the promptings of my own spirit.

Though I have labored to stitch my testimony into a coherent whole, my Didakhe consists of many parts, none of which you or any spirit need accept, for they are not Dogmata but Kerygmata.

Even if a spirit were to accept certain parts of my testimony, still then that spirit could reject other parts, for although I personally find that the corpus of my Didakhe all together—and only all together—satisfies the Desiderata, another spirit may wish to keep only certain parts.

Regard neither this testimony nor any other testimony—even those testimonies called "scripture"—as Dogma to be received as sacrosanct and elevated beyond questioning or criticism, perhaps to be treated with the obsessive devotion of fundamentalism, for all testimonies—even all so-called "scriptures"—come from but individual human spirits; all of it is of human origin and derived from and dependent upon human authority and Experience.

I have chosen to remain anonymous in my authorship of this work for that very reason, namely, that my testimony is like any other human testimony, the worth of which derives from not the identity of the author but the quality of the work.

Here my testimony ends at present, though it expresses only a small part of the Apokalypsis I have received and continue to receive from the Genius and Guru within me; my testimony shall continue to grow, develop, and change, for the Experience of my spirit, the ultimate source of my Apokalypsis and even of my

Gnosis and Suneidesis, all through my Higher Powers, will remain ever imperfect and limited.

I will issue new editions of my testimony for so long as I am inspired to do so, for the convictions of my spirit demand that I revise my words when I find them to be in error.

My testimony set forth in this work is the first to outline the New Living Tradition, itself the first blossom of a Pagan Reformation, but I hope that my testimony will not be the last, the fullest, or the greatest on the subject of Reform Paganism.

I hope that many other spirits—perhaps even you—will give their testimonies about a nascent family of Reform Pagan traditions of which this New Living Tradition is but the first, both while I am speaking and after my voice has fallen silent, so that my testimony may be complemented and corrected, so that the Pagan Reformation may continue in unceasing evolution, and so that this movement may one day bring the Pagan Restoration, through which humanity's Old Religion regains its former position among all humankind.

Until then, may this New Living Tradition and all Reform Pagan traditions guide, help, and encourage many persons toward Perfection:

May we ground ourselves in Nature's Creation; may we build interpersonal community in Love; may we glimpse the consilience of Truth; may we conform our whole lives to Will; and may we embrace spiritual life on spiritual paths of our own choosing up the Mount of Divine Ascent so that we may continue to participate in and facilitate the spiritual development of individual persons and the Autopoiesis of the entire Universe.

Blessed be.

Codicil
Additional Resources

You can learn more about the Pagan Reformation, connect with Reform Pagans, and explore Reform Paganism's growing family of traditions at ReformPagan.org.

You can learn more about the New Living Tradition and connect with our community at NewLivingTradition.org.

ReformPagan.org and NewLivingTradition.org are ministries of the New Living Foundation, which also publishes the works, including this one, under the New Living Classics imprint. You can learn more about the New Living Foundation and see a list of published and forthcoming titles at NewLivingFoundation.org.

〰︎

www.ingramcontent.com/pod-product-compliance
Lightning Source LLC
Chambersburg PA
CBHW061330040426
42444CB00011B/2848